MAKING A FORTUNE IN
CANADIAN STOCKS

MAKING A FORTUNE IN CANADIAN STOCKS

HOW TO GET STARTED ON THE ROAD TO WEALTH WITH CANADIAN EQUITIES

Patrick Doucette

Writers Club Press

San Jose New York Lincoln Shanghai

Making a Fortune in Canadian Stocks
How to get started on the road to wealth with Canadian equities

Writers Club Press
an imprint of iUniverse.com, Inc.

For information address:
iUniverse.com, Inc.
5220 S 16th, Ste. 200
Lincoln, NE 68512
www.iuniverse.com

The information contained is this book gives advice on the buying and
selling of equities; an activity which involves risk. This publication is
designed to provide accurate and authoritative information in regard to the
subject matter covered. It is sold with the understanding that the publisher is
not engaged in rendering legal, accounting, or other professional services. If
legal advice or other expert assistance is required, the services of a
competent professional person should be sought.

ISBN: 0-595-14697-X

Dedicated to Canadians
in search of their place in the sun.

Contents

Foreword

Many people state flatly, "I don't know anything about stocks or investing." If you've picked up this book, it must indicate that at least you have the desire to learn. It is hard to imagine an area that requires so little study and yet gives such huge returns as does learning how to handle your finances yourself.

Some people say, "I don't know anything about computers." Often they will spend months of study to learn about computers. Have you ever taken a course in Computer Network Administration? I have and can tell you firsthand, it is difficult and can be extremely complicated. Personal finance is not computer networking. It is enjoyable, rewarding and pretty easy to learn. Don't be put off by the concepts in this book that may at first glance appear to be complex. The ideas presented are basic common sense principles that anyone can understand. Be patient and willing to learn and you won't be disappointed.

Acknowledgements

I would like to acknowledge the kind support of family and friends without whose help I could not have written this book. In particular Judy and Kevin for their gracious hospitality and encouragement. Thanks to Brian Tracy for teaching me about setting goals and allowing me to share these ideas in this book. I would also like to acknowledge the kind co-operation of Data Broadcasting Corporation for allowing me to reprint their technical charts.

Introduction

The Internet is allowing more and more investors to make there own investment decisions by directly participating in the buying and selling of stocks. As individuals hear of the outstanding returns available to them by investing in specific equities, they are jumping online to take advantage of the opportunity. While it is quite simple to get started, there seems to be a bit of a void when it comes to the more concrete principles of buying and selling stocks, what should an investor buy and why? When should they sell? How can one avoid losing money? How can one spot the next hot stock? It is with these questions in mind that I have set out to write broad based information for the average Canadian investor. The content covered will range from the absolute basics to advanced strategies of market timing. Not everything written will be of benefit to everyone, however if the reader is able to employ just a few of the concepts presented and learn from them, I feel I will have accomplished what I have set out to achieve.

Handling one's own personal finances can be extremely rewarding and it is this theme that can be found throughout this book. The reader should sense that he or she is being encouraged with the words, "You can do it!" Keep this book as a reference and return to it often until the concepts are fully understood. So without further delay, let's get started....

Patrick Doucette   July, 2000

1

My Start

If thou faint in the day of adversity, thy strength is small.

Prov. 24 10

Alone in my pod, I sat and stared at my 5-year Anniversary Plaque of Loyal Service to the company. It had just been presented to me from some executive at the weekly company sales meeting. I was surprised to feel a twinge of pride inside; I am not sure if it was from an actual sense of accomplishment, the warm contented feeling of being publicly acknowledged or whether I was just pleased with myself at having survived five years without getting fired.

In any event, I knew that this milestone heralded a significant turning point in my life, I was 34 years old, laden with typical debts, mortgage, car, credit-cards etc…and still felt zero job security. Had it actually been 5 years already? I remember looking at old credit card statements of when I first came to Toronto to find work; the outstanding balances had not changed, I seemed to be in a permanent state of financial slavery with no significant change in sight.

Of course, it was not that I hadn't tried; from my early twenties I had never stopped struggling to get ahead with various ventures, many self-employed business attempts, glorious forays into network marketing, buying this or selling that…some had limited success but nothing ever seemed to really connect. The start-up costs usually ended up out-weighing the over-estimated returns, leaving me worse off than before I had started.

Still, I remained optimistic and it wasn't long afterwards that I walked into my local bank to ask for a loan. I had been reading books by people like Brian Tracy and Jim Rohn and began to realize that if I was ever going to get ahead, it would require concrete action on my part; especially in relation to investing. Years earlier I had graduated with a degree in Commerce thinking that an RRSP was a government ploy to get more taxes out of me; either University didn't teach me what I needed to know or I didn't pay much attention in class; probably a com-bination of the two.

I had read in a newspaper ad that I could borrow against my unused RSP contribution amount, and place the funds into a self-direct RRSP; the goal being-to earn a greater return that what I was being charged in interest and get a tax refund to boot. (I'll explain this in detail later.) So I walked into my local bank and confidently told the manager that I would like to apply for a carry-forward loan. Of course, the banker in question had no idea what I was talking about so I had to refer them to the newspaper ad. Coming from corporate culture myself, I understood perfectly that marketing departments do not always communicate their intentions to the poor saps having to deal directly with the customer.

To make a short story even shorter, I borrowed $15,000 and through investing in Canadian equities, watch it grow to over $250,000 in a mat-ter of about 18 months Not exactly a fortune but not too shabby either; my net worth has been steadily increasing ever since. Actually the opportunity to build a fortune is greater today than when I started. Now that I have the necessary "seed money" to invest with; the returns are better than ever, even through the severe market correction in April 2000. As examples, over the past two months, I have closed trades netting over $15,000 in one week and another $22,000 in three weeks. All while keeping risk to a minimum, maintaining large cash positions and keeping losses negligible.

Were these returns a fluke? Was it a random guess at picking a few good stocks? I would like to answer that question by detailing to you, dear reader, the steps I took and continue to take in evaluating whether a stock is or is not a good investment, both fundamentally and technically. It is my earnest hope that I can pass on to you some valuable insights that I have learned through my own personal investing experience; and in so doing help contribute towards your own financial success.

Having tried numerous ventures in my short lifetime, I can confidently assert how effective investing really is. Where else can you quickly acquire direct ownership in a business that is up and running, producing profits and rewarding investors on an ongoing basis? And all this with nominal transaction costs. To get a business off the ground, you need to invest in capital. You need to purchase office supplies; inventory or perhaps you need to advertise. Maybe you would need to invest $3000 to $5000 just for a small home office set-up. It could take you months and ten times that amount in revenues just to break even. That same $3000–$5000 can be put to work in a business that is already successfully established with no extra capital outlay on your part. You can see that same investment grow steadily month after month, year after year.

A more marked example would be the concept of buying a franchise. The name, goodwill and capital investment for some franchises could be $100,000 or much higher. The initial investment could take years to recoup. If the Toronto Stock Exchange charged $100,000 for the right to buy shares in the successful companies that are listed, I think it would be worth it. Yet access to the TSE is free! To purchase a franchise location of Canadian Tire for example could cost an investor $400,000. That same $400,000 invested in shares of Canadian

Tire Corporation in January 1997 would be worth $1,000,000 by January of 1999. Plus the holder of those shares would have also received $8,000 per year in dividend income. No sixteen-hour days, no worrying about inventory levels, no employee relations headaches; just sitting back and letting your money make money for you. Who is getting a better deal in this scenario, the franchisee or the shareholder? Certainly the shareholder is in better shape. However the shareholder must do their homework to be able to take advantage of such invest-ment opportunities and that is where this book will focus.

Before starting I must confess that my investing experience has been confined to a short period of history that has been characterized by a sustained bull market. But I have also experienced a 35% plunge in the stock market during April of 2000 where many speculative Internet based companies have dropped in value by over 80% and have yet to recover. In spite of this, by following basic common sense principles, I have avoided unnecessary losses and kept risk to a minimum. This same unprecedented opportunity is available to all Canadians and will richly reward those that are willing to seek out the right companies and stick to correct and disciplined trading methods.

2

Laying a Foundation

Love not sleep, lest thou come to poverty. Open thine eyes, and thou shalt be satisfied with bread.

Prov. 20 13

It is surprising to encounter so many successful hard-working individuals who seem to be diligent in all respects but if you were to pose them this question: "How are your financial investments doing?" they would look at you as if you were from another planet. Most people would mumble something to the effect of, "Oh, I have some mutual funds, you know, but I don't think about that kind of stuff." If they are not outright offended that you breached the taboo subject of personal finances, they will at the very least try and steer the topic away to something more tasteful like religion or politics. It is not surprising that this typical head-in-the-sand approach is common, however attitudes are slowly starting to change.

An entire generation of Canadians are starting to realize that we as a nation can be competitive in the areas of technology and the production of goods and services on a global scale; and because of this ability to produce products for our fellow world citizens, we have the opportunity to fully participate in the process and reap the ensuing benefits of world commerce.

After all, what does it mean to be wealthy? Wealth can be defined as ownership of the factors of production. If you are able to dig a ditch with your bare hands you are not wealthy, if you own a backhoe that can dig a ditch, you have acquired a certain amount of wealth...you own capital that can produce a good or service that can be exchanged for MONEY. To be wealthy means you own capital. If you own a bunch of stuff; cars, boats, planes etc, it does not necessarily mean that you are wealthy. It may mean that you are severely in debt. If you own cars that taxi people to and fro, if you own boats that take people on cruises and if you own planes that transport cargo then you have a certain amount of capital; you have a certain amount of wealth....get it? Good, let's move on.

As long as you stay in your cubicle, punch your clock, and live paycheck to paycheck, your prospects for accumulating wealth are zero, plain and simple, wealth is not going to appear from nowhere. Well what about my pension plan? Yes, that's a start but let's elaborate a little. When you save a few bucks and start to buy stocks, an amazing transformation happens; you are no longer a corporate drone, suddenly you are a part owner of a company. However small it may be, when you purchase an equity interest in a public company, that is, you buy that company's shares; you immediately become a part owner of the assets, the capital, of that firm.

How is this possible? Isn't the stock market just like going to a casino, isn't it all just a gamble? Let's back track a bit...let me tell you a little story.

Let's say Edger starts his own little widget company and he is the one out of ten that does not fail (the business jungle has a delightful way of weeding out ventures that are unnecessary). Well suddenly Edger gets an order from Widget Retail Inc for a gazillion of his widgets, everyone wants one in a real hurry. Can Edger do all the production himself from his basement? No he needs capital, he needs more employees and more manufacturing equipment to meet demand. He goes to the banks for money to expand and they say,

"Get out of here, can't you see we're busy collecting services charges from the working drones!"

So Edger is stuck, what can he do? He decides to go to all his friends and borrow $1000 from each of them. But since he not very popular, he only has two friends and that is just not enough, he needs millions. So he decides to go to the money river, also called the stock market and meet with some guys in suits called underwriters. These underwriters are very popular and have lots and lots of friends. Edgar explains his predicament and the underwriter's say,

"We will contact all our friends and get you the money you need; in exchange we will charge you a commission based on how much money we raise. You will have to give a portion of the ownership of your company to our friends in return for their money ".

When the friends, also called investors, give their money, they get shares in return, each share representing a part ownership in Edger's company. When the investors want to trade their shares back and forth, they do so on the stock exchange. Isn't that simple? What about the risk you ask? Yes, well the risk is there all right. Edger might accidentally burn down his manufacturing plant, or people might stop wanting his widgets. That would cause the value of the shares in his company to fall. However if the demand for his widgets remains strong, his company may prosper, produce profits for the shareholders and the value of the stocks may increase.

Now there may be some Edger's out there who go to the money river without actually having a real company; but since they are good friends with the underwriters, they pretend to have a company, get lots of money and then leave town. That is where the risk of buying stocks becomes glaringly obvious. You need to get a reasonably accurate picture of what is going on with the widget company and what kind of character Edger happens to be.

And this is where you come into the picture. You have been faithfully saving 10% of your income and depositing it into your bank account, hoping it does not get eaten up by all the service charges. After much struggle and self-sacrifice you have $5000 with which to begin your journey towards untold wealth. You meet Edger a little while after he has raised his money and he tells you how excited he is about how many widgets he is going to produce and how much money his company is going to make. He tells you that even though you were not one of his original friends, you can still go to the money river and buy some of the stocks in his company by asking for the stock ticker symbol WDGT.

Full of greed induced euphoria, you rush down to the money river and buy 5000 shares of WDGT for the offered price $1.00 each; WOW! You are now a part owner in Edgar's company. That night you have the best nights sleep in a long time as you snugly envision your capital at work for you 24hrs a day. You can see the shifts of workers arriving at the plant and envision scores of widgets coming off the assembly lines.

The next day at your 9 to 5 job, you breeze through the usual grind with renewed vigor fuelled by the knowledge of the fact that you now have capital, you now own some factors of production, yessir…long live free enterprise. You are no longer a corporate drone; instead you are a humanitarian, humbly serving your fellow citizens by providing the noble widget to young and old alike.

Several months later you read in your local newspaper that the Acme Widget Company wants to buy all of Edger's company so they can corner the market and mercilessly raise the price of Widgets to earn more profits, they boldly announce that they will offer to buy every last one of Edger's company shares (including yours!) for $5 each. You return to the money river and sell your shares for 5 times what you paid. You now have $25000 in cash and are beside yourself with joy. Isn't that a nice little story?

That is about as basic as it gets. Yes the stock market can be risky, yes the stock market can be like gambling but only if YOU treat it that way.

The stock market is a place where you can INVEST in a particular company by buying a share(s) in that company. As a shareholder you can participate in the success (and failure) of any public company on any exchange. If you want to throw darts at the financial pages to select stocks then your returns will indeed be random. If you want to sympathize with the title of this book then open your mind and don't accept the cynical mindsets that are all too common.

The ending of our little story is unfortunately, a little on the wishful thinking side. The ending we are looking for is one in which Edgar's company continues to experience strong demand for their widgets with healthy profit margins, resulting in a steady increase in net earnings and a corresponding steady increase in share prices. That is what you will be looking for when selecting which stocks to invest in; you will by no means need to rely only on luck.

So to sum up, the first step to getting started is to have a basic understanding of what the stock market is all about. A great book on the background of the stock market is The Golden Fleece by Walter Stewart, I would highly recommend this book since it gives the reader an awareness of the dangers inherent in the stock market. Unfortunately it is out of print on Internet bookseller lists but is probably available from your local library.

The second step is the process of opening a trading account. This is a no-brainer and can easily be accomplished by speaking to your local bank manager for help. All the major banks offer accounts that allow you to buy and sell stocks. There are also discount brokers online that do not have a retail banking presence in Canada. I have listed both types of online brokers in the Appendix at the back of this book. Personally I use TD Waterhouse and find the service to be convenient. Information on opening an investment/trading account is readily available to anyone connected to the web. You can also inquire at your local bank branch if you get stuck.

One small caveat to remember is that financial institutions can be notoriously slow in moving your money around. For example if you want to close a mutual fund, switch banks, transfer funds from a company pension etc, give yourself a good four weeks or more to get things processed. Setting up a trading account is easy but getting the money in there can take some time!

I would recommend opening a self-directed RRSP as your primary trading account. There is nothing unusual about this, this type of account allows you to defer paying tax on you capital gains (stock profits) until you actually need to withdraw the funds. It is simply a convenient place to build tax-deferred profits. You can buy and sell stocks within this type of account the same as in a direct trading account. When you withdraw funds from this account, tax is withheld at a rate of 10% on withdrawals up to $5000, 15% on withdrawals up to $10,000 and 20% on withdrawal over $15,000. Your broker may charge an annual administration fee of $50 to $100 per year on self-direct trading account with less than $25,000 in them. (A motivation to grow your account above this level!)

You are also restricted from trading on margin in this type of account. Trading on margin is where you borrow up to 50% of the cash used to trade from your bank or broker. This allows you to leverage for faster gains but also accelerates losses when the market goes against you. (Not a good idea as will be discussed later). If you have difficulty with the concept of a self-direct RSP trading account you can still open a regular direct trading account (cash account).

There seems to be a common belief that money in an RRSP is 'untouchable' due to negative tax consequences. I withdraw $5000 per month from my Self-Direct RRSP and 10% is withheld at source and submitted to Revenue Canada on my behalf. No problem there. At the end of the year, I receive T4 statements and process my tax return as normal. Depending on my expenses for the year I will have roughly the same tax bill or refund as when I worked as a commission salesperson. Don't worry that somehow your funds in an RRSP are not accessible.

You simply phone the brokerage service you deal with and ask to transfer however much of the cash portion you need to your regular bank account. The funds are transferred usually with 24 to 48 hrs. The myth of not being able to touch RRSP money is simply perpetuated by people that don't like to pay taxes. Yes you will be taxed at your marginal tax rate at the end of the year but the funds are easily accessible nonetheless. Simply plan your tax payments accordingly.

Don't forget where the RRSP came from. Years back, the government commissioned a study to find out why a lot of Canadians were retiring with little or no means of self-support, having instead to rely on their government pension or working relatives for meager subsistence. After much study they found out, lo and behold, the reason people retire poor is that they do not save during their working years; quite profound. Anyway, to try and correct this potential drain on the economy, the wise politicians of that time said,

"Let's give the citizens of Canada an incentive to save money during their working years so that they don't starve when they retire and end up having to be supported in old age by the government."

Some extremely sharp chap responded,

"Why don't we tell the citizens that if they save money and put it in a savings account, they won't have to pay any tax on that money, in fact we could give them back the taxes we deducted off that money as a kind of refund incentive."

"Great idea, chap, what shall we call this program?"

"Let's call it a registered retirement survival plan".

They all agreed that was a great idea and as the paperwork was processed the name ended up getting changed to Registered Retirement Savings Plan but personally I prefer the original name.

YOUR NOTICE OF ASSESSMENT

Now, every year if you are a diligent drone, you will receive from Revenue Canada a form called: Notice of Assessment. That is if you filed a tax return, you get sent this Notice of Assessment which outlines your revenue, taxes paid and RRSP contributions; now take special note of the line that states: unused RRSP deduction limit at the end of (year) as well the last line which shows: **RRSP deduction limit for (current calendar year)** ...this is your magic number! One strategy is to pay a visit to your local bank and tell them you want to make a loan for this amount amortized over as long a period as possible, preferably fifteen years. (You will actually plan to pay this back much sooner.) Now unless you've been bankrupt a half dozen times in the last 5 years, there is probably not a bank in Canada that would refuse this loan request. Why? Because the loan is guaranteed by the RSP deposit itself! You get, say $15,000 from your bank, you deposit this money into a self-direct RRSP (and promise not to take it out right away!) and you get a huge tax refund for that taxation year to boot! Your loan is in a way partially underwritten by the Government of Canada! Lets look at how this can work:

Start	Borrow $15,000	Deposit $15,000 Into Self Direct RRSP Account	Tax Refund (40%)	Cumulative Net Worth Gain
Initial Result	Owe -$15,000	Self Direct RRSP Accnt+$15,000	Tax Refund $6,000	$6,000
End of Year 1	Owe -$14545*	Self Direct RRSP Account=$21,000*		$12,455
End of Year 2	Owe -$14042	Self Direct RRSP Account=$29,400*		$21,358

1) Assuming loan is at 10% interest rate, 15 year amortization, payments=$161.00/month

* Assuming you can achieve 40% annual return on your investments

That's how it CAN work, if you are willing to sign your name on some forms, you can instantly gain $6,000 or more depending on your marginal tax rate...just for taking on the loan and assuming the risk. The banks **need** you to take the risk. They want your signature... why...because for them, it is a low risk loan and that is what they do to make money; they lend money. How risky is it for you? Could you lose all your money in your self-direct account by investing in Bre-X and then be stuck with a huge loan to payoff? Yes. Could you keep your self-direct funds in GIC'S and endure zero risk for the life of the loan (an effective method of forced saving)? Absolutely. Could you earn greater than a 40% annual return and end up paying off your RRSP Loan much sooner than anticipated? Yes. In fact following the example above, I have long since paid off my original RRSP loan and am left with a Self-Direct RRSP account which continues to grow steadily.

If you can somehow afford to manage monthly payments of $161.00, a person would have to be insane not to take advantage of this opportunity. You can maintain any level of risk that is comfortable for you while getting an instant tax refund bonus. In fact, if you made the loan in December, you would only have to make about four or five payments before getting your tax refund to use for further payments! Or you could use your tax refund to immediately pay down your RRSP Carry-Forward loan, which is open-ended (no penalty for paying off early).

Even if you borrow $15,000 at 10% interest, make your monthly payments of $161 per month and put the entire proceeds into GIC's offering 5% interest. At the end of 15 years you would have paid off the loan and be left with an RRSP account with $31,183.00... not too bad. In comparison if you borrow $15,000 to buy a new car, you will have hefty payments of $380 per month; pay off the car in 4 years and at the end of ten years, your car is worth zero! You are left with absolutely nothing and during those four years of payments, you will probably be living paycheck to paycheck. Which scenario is going to lead to wealth?

This is **the difference between good debt and bad debt.** Reread this paragraph a few times until you thoroughly understand when it can be a good idea to borrow and when it isn't.

By the way, if you actually could consistently get an annual return of 40% on your initial $15,000 investment, your RRSP would have grown to over 2.3 million after 15 years! Before you scream, "That's impossible!" Consider the fact that there are people that can verify over 100% annual returns for the last four years in a row. Anything is possible, right?

I cannot over-emphasize the previous point about good and bad debt, especially for those just starting out in the workplace. As soon as Mr. or Mrs. fresh graduate gets that new white-collar position, they run to the car dealership for the hip upwardly mobile bad-debt vehicle, which is like voluntarily putting on a pair of financial handcuffs. That combined with the expensive apartment and the money misery is complete. Ten years go by and the fresh faced idealist is now 30 years old with credit cards maxed out, a kid on the way and a car that's on it's last legs. I'll get off my soapbox for now and return later.

Now what if the person has no RRSP deduction limit? Then either you always max out your RRSP contributions each year; in which case you don't really need to be reading this book since you are well on the way to abundant prosperity without my help; or you have not been in the workforce long enough, if at all. In this case, go get a job for a few years to get an appreciation of misery and then come back and read this book. For the vast majority of Canadians out there, it is likely that they have plenty of unused RRSP contribution room, which is just waiting to be discovered. If you take advantage of the example above, **make sure you read this book completely before doing anything with your investment funds!** You are now in business and must take your investing seriously if you are to succeed.

For a lot of other people, running down to the local bank is not possible. Due to an aversion to any kind of debt or perhaps negative past experience, borrowing to invest is simply not an option. For these people, the only method is to save up some investment funds. In today's economy, unemployment is at historically low levels. Since there is always residual unemployment to some degree (4%-5% due to people transitioning from one job to the next) you could almost say we are at full employment. That is anyone willing and able to work can find work of some kind. Once you have a job and a clear idea of how much cash you have coming in, it simply remains to forcibly set aside a specific amount every month for your investment account. We'll look at this priority again a little later.

For now let's assume you have either diligently saved up that initial $5000 to $15000 in cash and have deposited it to your trading account. Or you have borrowed it like in the example given above. What's next?

3

Why Canadian, Eh?

Better is an handful with quietness, than both the hands full with travail and vexation of spirit.

Eccles. 4 v 6

Many investors derisively scoff, "There's no opportunity in Canadian stocks, I only trade on the NASDAQ." I would disagree with this negative generalization for several reasons.

First, as an individual investor you will need to thoroughly examine specific publicly traded companies before plunking down your hard earned cash. This requires time. The TSE currently lists about 1400 different companies. The NASDAQ lists well over 5000. The simple limitations of a persons time makes analysis of the NASDAQ market almost four times as difficult.

Second, if you invest in a Canadian company that is healthy and growing, it will often take out a listing on a U.S. exchange eventually anyway; in effect allowing you to invest at a discount before it hits U.S. investors and the associated rise in stock price.

Third, there are often exchange rate considerations and greater difficulty in order fulfillment when purchasing stocks traded on U.S. exchanges.

Fourth, there can be significant tax advantages to purchasing Canadian stocks. If you limit your stocks purchase to mostly (80%) Canadian equities, then you can trade within a self-direct RSP as mentioned previously and temporarily defer the payment of tax on your capital gains.

Finally the TSE300 has recently begun to surpass the performance of the U.S. indexes. Mutual fund investors will be familiar with the mantra "Maximize your foreign content, maximize your foreign content" It should be self evident to the reader that this advice is passé, irrelevant or whatever else you want to call it. If you want to maximize your returns, maximize your Canadian content! Yes, the Canadian market is a small fraction of the global marketplace but it is a market that you can safely investigate. If you want pick stocks on the Nasdaq, Nikkei or Hang Seng go ahead but don't forget the diamonds in your own backyard. By telling an investor, "You should have more global diversification", you are implying that there are pathetically few opportunities in little old Canada.....dead wrong. I would caution investors to avoid investing in areas that they know nothing about unless they want to lose money in a hurry. Canada has more than enough public companies that are experiencing solid double-digit growth on a year over year basis.

Even though a single company heavily influences the TSE300; (Nortel Networks is currently worth about 34% of the index[1]) the entire high technology industry in Canada is rapidly growing. Particularly in Ottawa, Toronto, Kitchener-Waterloo region, Vancouver

---

1. Canadian Business, Aug 21st, 2000 pp.31-33

and even Calgary. Many public companies from these areas are experiencing tremendous growth and many others will be going public in the near future.

A word about what exchange to trade on. I would suggest to the reader to limit their choices to the 1400 or so companies listed on the Toronto stock exchange. Stocks also trade on the CDNX also known appropriately as the Canadian Venture Exchange. About 2400 companies are listed on the CDNX. The Canadian Venture Exchange is the result of the merging of the Vancouver and Alberta stock exchanges. I have bought and sold shares on these exchanges with the understanding that a) the shares listed are usually of a higher risk than companies listed on the TSE b) the bid and ask of these shares can be quite wide and volatile; combined with the fact that they are often thinly traded can result in difficulty in buying and selling to your benefit. Are there good solid companies listed on the CDNX? Yes. Are they difficult to find and trade profitably? Yes.

To determine if you are a candidate to buy stocks on the CDNX, take this simple test:

1) Do you think that motorcycles are safe?
2) Are you under the age of 25?
3) Do you enjoy extreme sports like skateboarding on hand railings?
4) Would you say that slot machines are fun?
5) Do you feel that blackjack gives pretty good odds for making a quick buck?
6) When you buy a coffee, instead of getting your change back, do you sometimes accidentally yell at the waitress, "LET IT RIDE, SISTER!"…?

If you answer YES to any of the above questions, you probably have the fortitude to trade on the CDNX, you may even make some profits. Seriously, there are good companies to be found that can produce outstanding returns but you will have to dig twice as hard to get the solid information you need to trade and/or invest wisely. In particular look for companies that are planning to get listed on the TSE in the near future. I purchased Wi-Lan (TSE: WIN) when it was trading on the Alberta exchange for $8 and watched it rise nicely as it migrated to the TSE , but remember that for every Wi-Lan there are probably many, many more under-performing stocks.

Always keep in mind that for a lot of companies on the CDNX, especially concept or idea companies; their main goal is to raise cash. Once they have raised money by floating an issue, they can get down to the business of trying to produce and or expand their ideas. The commitment to shareholders in the form of profits and or a rising share price in the short term can be essentially non-existent. It is your job to find out what the goals of management are. This will be discussed further in the chapter on fundamental analysis.

So for the sake of the beginning Canadian investor let's assume that we will be staying with companies listed on the Toronto Stock Exchange. Take some time to visit www.tse.com to see what information is available to you there.

MUTUAL FUNDS

It should be obvious to the reader that this is not a book about mutual funds. Mutual funds can perhaps maintain your investment but will they make you rich? Before looking at the published returns and all the good press on mutual funds, seek out someone who has actually been holding funds over a few years and ask them what kind of returns they have experienced. If you are happy with their answer, by all means go crazy. You may get lucky and be able to achieve 10% to 20% or more return on investment annually.

Realize that most Canadian equity mutual funds under perform the TSE300 index. A recent ranking of the top 50 Canadian small-mid cap equity growth funds showed three had returns above 30% over a three-year period; two had three-year returns of over 20 %; ten had three-year returns between 10% and 20%, twenty-seven had returns below 10% and the rest had negative returns over a three-year period. And this was for the top 50 out of 133 to choose from!

For regular Canadian Equity Funds the top 50 showed two funds had 3-year returns over 30%; three had three-year returns between 20% and 30% and forty-five had returns between 10% and 20%. And this also was for the top 50 out of 358 funds! What if you happened to pick funds not in the top 50? Seventy-four of the 358 funds listed had returns below 10%, eleven had negative returns and the rest did not have a three-year track record.[2]

Are you comfortable with the performance listed above? I didn't make these numbers up; they are publicly available to anyone interested. Why does it seem that newspapers ads for some funds boast huge returns but they don't appear on independent survey results? Why is it that so few funds have a three-year track record? A mutual fund will get astounding returns one year and then self-destruct; the funds are often re-named and shuffled so they start afresh with no history. **For an investment vehicle that is intended to reduce the risk of purchasing stocks through diversification and professional management, the fundamental information I have found on Canadian equity mutual funds leads me to believe that they are moderate-risk investments with a low probability of producing consistent returns above 10% annually.** My own calculation would indicate that the Canadian equity mutual fund investor has about a 1 in 10 to about a 1 in 8 chance of selecting an equity mutual fund that will consistently achieve returns above 10% annually.

There is plenty of information available on how to select mutual funds. You would be better off with mutual funds invested in bonds or

2. Globefund Canadian Mutual Fund Ranking , Sept 3, 2000 www.globefund.com

mortgages. Don't forget, you face the same risk of market downturns with equity mutual funds as you do in selecting your own stocks. The risk should actually be less for the disciplined stock trader since he or she will be heavily invested in cash for significant periods of time.

This book is focused on profitably buying Canadian stocks for the right reasons so before we begin, let look at some bad reasons to buy stocks.

4

Top Ten Worst (and most common) Reasons to Buy a Stock

He that is slothful in his work is brother to him that is a great waster.

Prov. 18 v 9

Before getting into Fundamental Analysis I would like to look at a few common errors as to why people select stocks.

10) My friend told me this was a good stock.

This reason can take many forms. My friend knows someone who works there and they said the stock is going to go up. My friend works for a company that is going to be bought out, my friend this, my friend that. The idea of relying on your friends defeats the underlying concept of managing your own finances. Whether your friend is right or wrong about a company will be dependant upon the information that is available to you directly. These are PUBLIC companies that we are talking about. The reason they are called public is because the financial information must be made available to the public on a quarterly basis. If your friend has genuine inside information, you don't want to be trading based on that because a) it is illegal–unless you like the idea of being arrested and fined don't listen to any "hot" inside information. And b) by the time the information has reached you it is, in all likelihood, old news and already factored into the stock price. Let's face it; unless you regularly have lunch with CEO's and play golf with the president of the TSE, it is doubtful that you will hear any market making news before it is released through normal channels. If your friend tells you about a stock, thank him or her for the lead and then do your own research. There are no shortcuts.

9) I read a positive article on this company in the newspaper.

Newspapers can often provide solid fundamental information that can help you make sound trading decisions but be careful; a front page spread in the business section is usually a better indication for you to take profits than to make a purchase. Always try and read between the lines. Is the information presented dealing strictly with financial information? Is it referring to potential or confirmed orders? Take a look at the stocks recent trading activity in the area of volume and price. Has the stock risen in anticipation of this news release? If so, you can be sure that profit taking will drive the price down.

8) The price of the stock is cheap.

"The shares are trading at only $2.00, I think it's a good deal!"
"XYZ Company is trading at $85.00 per share. Oh my, that's too high!"
"The cost is only $1.00 per share, it can't go any lower than that!"
All these types of comments give an indication of a basic lack of understanding of share value. The value of a stock is dependant upon the number of shares outstanding in relation to the overall worth of a company. If there is only one share outstanding and you can buy it (the

whole company) for $85, would that still be considered expensive? Of course not, the number of shares outstanding must be examined to determine the market capitalization. The value of a share is related to tangible assets (book value), as well intangible such as future prospects, goodwill, market sentiment, etc. The actual quoted price is totally arbitrary and can only be considered "cheap" or "expensive" by examining many factors, not just the price itself. Also, always remember a stock can move from $100 to $200 just as fast as a stock can go from $1 to $2 and same thing on the way down, got it?

7) The price of the stock is at a low point.

Similar to reason number eight. Before trying to pick the "bottom" on stocks, ask yourself this: how have the investors who have been holding the stock for a year been treated? Have they experienced solid returns? If so than you may be buying on a dip, however if the stock has been steadily dropping, it will most likely continue to steadily drop; don't look for a turnaround but rather get on board with a steadily rising stock. Don't rely on a stock to "bounce back".

6) My broker said it was on his recommended "buy" list.

Never purchase a stock based on a telephone conversation. Look at the published numbers in writing yourself. Brokers can give good advice, brokers can give bad advice. Why let someone else do your thinking for you? I'm not writing with a grudge to bash brokers but you don't have to look very far to find published stories of mismanaged accounts, "churning" and or other questionable practices.

5) It's a hot new IPO.

A new listing, (Initial Public Offering) is not a guarantee of success. When a stock starts trading on the TSE, it will often have an initial spike followed by a significant drop; which is not surprising since the IPO itself is often sold at the best of conditions and is aggressively marketed. Once the initial "hype" dies down after a few weeks or even months, you may be able to pick up the same shares at a discount if you have fundamental reasons for doing so, not just because it is new.

4) The clinical trials/geological surveys are showing positive results.

I'll let you in on a secret....all mining companies listed on the TSE have discovered tons of gold and acres of diamonds and all biotech companies have discovered a cure for cancer and an elixir for immortality. That's right, each and every one. Now that you know this beforehand, you can get on with examining the companies prospects for profits based on production capability and act accordingly.

3) I like the name of the company.

Don't be swayed because the company name sounds nice. The company name has no effect on whether it will prosper or not. Brand names for consumers is a different issue altogether. I don't want to belabor this point since it should be self-evident.

2) I have a good feeling about this company.

This is the number one reason for holding onto a dog stock. Many investors fall in love with a particular company and continue to believe despite evidence to the contrary that they are always on the verge of a great breakthrough that will propel their stock to dizzying heights of greatness. To avoid this error try not to rely on any upcoming news, new developments, new breakthroughs etc. A winning stock is not going to be some great surprise to everyone but you. Invest in a solid company and you will get solid returns. There is no room for hoping, wishing, thinking or feeling in the world of investing.

1) I don't care if the price goes down.

This is by far the worst reason to buy a stock but surprisingly common. Very often you will hear someone say, "I'm just going to throw in five grand and not bother to watch it. I don't care if it goes down or not, I'm just going to let it sit there for the long term." Don't let these words come out of your mouth! You SHOULD care about whether your stocks go up or not. Your investment account is not a place to throw money; it is where you take purposeful action based on research. There is certainly a place for a buy and hold strategy, you buy and hold stocks that are consistently performing well; you don't buy a stock to watch it deteriorate into oblivion.

A word to the wise, at times you will no doubt hear your friends use some of these ten reasons to support their stock purchases. When this happens, try not to convince them otherwise. People are funny and easily offended especially when it comes to the decisions they are making about money. Maybe the best thing you can do is to suggest that they read this book. The written word has a way of hitting people over the head in a way that they will gladly accept and learn from; the same words coming from a neighbor over a backyard fence can cause no end of angry feelings and resentment.

5

Fundamental Analysis

If thou be wise, though shalt be wise for thyself: but is though scornest, thou alone shalt bear it.

Prov. 9 12

Two main ways of researching and evaluating a company are through Fundamental Analysis or Technical Analysis. Fundamental analysis is looking at the numbers, the projected sales of a company and it's profitability etc. Technical Analysis is the process of examining a shares price and volume history and analyzing the data with various methods in the hope of being able to predict future share price activity. Technical analysis is more of the crystal ball approach to be sure, but both methods deserve to be looked at closely.

First of all, don't be intimidated by the concept of trying to determine the financial soundness of a company. Many beginning investors have many questions and concerns about what all the numbers mean. It is kind of like someone sitting down in the cockpit of a 747 and trying to understand all the switches and gauges. What does this mean? What does this do? Meanwhile the pilot sits down and says, this is a piece of cake, and proceeds to fly the plane as easy as riding a bicycle. Investing in stocks is a lot easier than flying a 747 but it will take some study. The person who says: " Oh I could never understand all that financial stuff" is like the person who says, "Oh, I could never learn to drive a car". You don't really have to learn to drive a car, but if you don't, you are closing off a lot of opportunity and mobility to yourself. Learning to invest in stocks properly on your own involves about the same degree of difficulty as learning to drive a car. Intimidating at first, but very easy once you get the hang of it.

FINANCIAL STATEMENTS

To properly purchase shares in a publicly traded company you must not be intimidated by financial statements. This is not rocket science. You don't have to be a chartered accountant to understand if a company is doing well or not. (Although that certainly would not hurt either) Here is a sample company's **BALANCE SHEET:**

ASSETS	How much stuff they own including accounts receivable	$1,000,000
LIABILITIES	How much they owe including accounts payable	$500, 000
EQUITY	What's left, the difference between assets and liabilities	$500,000

Is that simple? The company above has some equity; there is some inherent value. Equity for a public company is called shareholder equity.

Things to remember when looking at a balance sheet:

1) Does the company have sufficient cash to support day-to-day operations?

2) Does the company have excessive debt? (Usually shown as long-term debt)

There are a few basic things to look for when looking at a company **INCOME STATEMENT:**

1) How much Revenue does the company have and is the Revenue increasing?

2) What is the Net Income (revenue minus expenses)?

3) Divide Net Income by Revenue to get Profit Margin.

Example: XYZ Company Income Statement

	1999	1998
Revenue	$1,000,000	$500,000
Expenses	$500,000	$250,000
Net Income (Profit)	$500,000	$250,000
# shares outstanding	1 million	1 million
Earnings per share	.50 cents	.25 cents
Share Price	$50	$25

For XYZ company above, you can see that profit margin is 50% (Net Income/Revenue). That is a very healthy profit margin.

A profit margin of 10% is a gauge, less than 10% is tight margins, less that 5% is very slim margins; above 10% is healthy, above 20% is fat margins. Simple right? If Net Income is negative, the company is losing money. Don't invest in a company that is losing money.

Price Earning Ratio=price of the stock divided by earnings per share. Let's say XYZ company shares are trading for $50 per share. Thus P/E Ratio=$50/.50 cents=100

What is a normal P/E Ratio? It depends on the expected growth of the company among other factors; basically it depends on what the market is willing to pay for a stock. Here is a very general guideline for P/E Ratios.

P/E Ratio =10   Established company annual growth about 10% per year.

P/E Ratio =50   Fast growing high-tech company growing at 40% per year

P/E Ratio =500   dot.com roller coaster, growth over 100%-volatile

Remember that a company's profitability or potential for profits is more important than the actual P/E ratio since some companies will have good prospects before having actual profits resulting in no computable P/E Ratio. A good mental exercise when looking at P/E ratios is to ask yourself, "Will **this particular company ever earn $1.00 per share?** How long will that take? One year? Two? At the current P/E ratio, what will the company share price be when it earns $1.00 per share? What is a reasonable P/E Ratio for the industry that this company is involved in?

For XYZ company listed above we see that the P/E ratio is 100, which is reasonable considering the company is growing at 100% annually and is maintaining high profit margins. A company such as XYZ Company could trade at such a price in today's stock market environment. A P/E ratio that is about equal to a company's rate of annual growth is usually considered normal.

Another ratio to look at for fast growing companies is market cap to revenue…(Market Capitalization/Revenue)=MC/R Ratio

For XYZ company, the **Market Capitalization (share price x number of shares outstanding)**=$50 x 1 million=$50 million. Thus XYZ company has a market cap to revenue ratio of 50 times. Market Capitalization should always be examined since it represents the total value of a company.

Would you buy XYZ Company for 50 million dollars if it were making profits of $500,000 per year, would you pay more or less? Traditionally an investor would be willing to buy a company for from one to ten times its annual revenues. (The purchase price would be related to profitability.) This is a valuable mental exercise and should be made a habit when looking at a company. When calculating market cap to revenue, you will want to compare the numbers to companies in a similar industry, i.e. their competitors. Compare this ratio to companies that are doing the same thing but are further along in their growth cycle as a company or those that are just starting out. Eventually you will start to get an idea of what a company is worth and whether its shares are consequently cheap or expensive. The only way to determine the relative "costs" of companies is by comparison.

When you are looking to buy a house and see one priced at $200,000 is that cheap or expensive? Well it depends right? It depends on the location, features and the relative cost of similar homes available on the market. Buying stocks in this regard is quite similar.... whether the stock is cheap or not depends on certain factors. Do you walk into a real estate office and say, I have this much money; what can I buy? Neither should you open a trading account and say o.k. I have this much money, how many shares can I buy? If the house you wanted sold on one day for $200,000 and the next day, the same house sold for $185,000, how careful would you be in purchasing it at the right time at a fair price? If you want to be serious about making money in stocks buy the house for $185,000 and the selling will take care of itself.

Again, the key thing to remember when looking at financial statements is don't be intimidated by them. Use common sense and look for increasing revenues with steady profit margins. As you examine and compare financial results from different companies you will start to get a better understanding of how a company is doing by looking at the financials. This can help strengthen your resolve when you are holding a stock long-term and are faced with a few minor market corrections.

When you know the fundamentals are strong, you won't get shaken out of your position at a bad time. If looking at a company on the TSE, always look it up on the TSE website and check the link 'financial snapshot' of the company in question. This will give you a quick uncomplicated view of recent financial fundamentals.

CONFERENCE CALLS & VISITS

I have yet to read in any book the benefits of participating in a company's conference calls. Either I don't read much or this is not often mentioned. In any event I want the reader to be aware of this vital source of information. Most firms on the TSE will hold a quarterly conference call to discuss their financial results with the investment community. You as an individual investor will be able to listen to a recorded version of the call shortly after the actual live call takes place. Always take advantage of this. It's free, takes an hour or two of your time but is worth every minute. Preferably have a speaker phone and with a pen and paper; take notes about what is being discussed. Write down any sales targets, forecasts or profit goals and do your own calculating. Based on what you hear, what are the chances that company will earn $1 per share? What is a reasonable P/E ratio for the company? Did management have difficulty in answering any tough questions?

Instructions on these calls will be openly published on Internet newswires so there will not be any difficulty in accessing the call. Not all companies open their calls to the public, but many do.

During these calls, management will discuss what they feel are the company's prospects for growth; this is an ideal opportunity for you to get a better feel for the company. It will give you a more personal connection to the company and strengthen your opinion on whether to buy the shares or not.

On a similar note, if you are able to attend a company's annual meeting, make sure you do. This can be an opportunity to meet the management, ask questions and get a feel for how dedicated they are towards the shareholders and how positive the company feels about the future. It will also increase your enthusiasm for investing.

This also holds true for actually paying a visit to the company you are interested in. How open is the company to allowing investors tour their facilities? Call or e-mail the investor relations person and ask them questions, don't waste their time but present a few straightforward questions and see what response you get. Some questions to ask include:

What is the current number of employees? When is next scheduled earnings release date? Does the company mail out an investor relations kit?

COMPANY WEBSITE

When looking at a company website try and get a feel for whether they are catering more to potential investors or potential customers.

In particular look at their careers section. Are there numerous openings or do they simply indicate an address to send in résumés. How hard are they trying to attract quality people? I recently invested in a company that was recruiting for a sales manager that could handle 50% annual growth sales targets. Was that a good indication of demand for the company's products? Absolutely! Needless to say, I was very happy with that investment. You can also check the Careers section in your local paper to see who is recruiting aggressively to meet demand.

A company's website should not be one huge advertisement to invest in their stock. Keep an eye open for links to their business partners or clients especially if they are supplying Fortune 500 companies.

Check that the recent financial statements are properly posted. Read the investor relations section and news releases to learn what is happening in the areas of new products, new management appointments, new contracts signed etc. Check if they have a prospectus available for download. This is an outline of all the pertinent facts on a company that is given prior to the issuance of an IPO (initial public offering).

The prospectus can provide fundamental information including risks facing the company. If a prospectus is available, always READ IT COMPLETELY!

A quick addendum on exploring the web for fundamental data, if possible, avoid reading discussion boards, stock chat rooms etc. In general these will be a waste of your time. Although you may get some useful feedback on occasion, by and large you will not be helped by monitoring inane banter by the average investor trying to make a buck. Message boards are usually filled with silly comments, incorrect information and generally unpleasant people. Stick to reliable sources for your information, like the company's own web site, reputable newswire services like Reuters, Canada Newswire etc.

An excellent site to access fundamental information is Yahoo Finance; it has links to research by Zack's Brokerage Research Reports and often gives a detailed profile for Canadian Stocks. Another great site is globeinvestor.com. There are numerous sites you can access for fundamental data and it becomes a matter of personal preference which sites you prefer. I list some useful sites at the end of this book that you can check out.

INSIDER TRADING REPORTS

Insider trading reports reveal share trades made by individuals that are considered to be "insiders"; they are usually the executives of a particular public company. When insiders buy or sell shares in their own company, the transactions are documented and published. You can find these documented in financial newspapers and on a variety of investment oriented websites. (See website list at end of book)

Insider transactions can be a good indication of where top management feels their shares are headed. (If insiders are buying, they anticipate the shares to go higher and if they are selling, they may feel that shares prices are headed lower.) Firstly remember that even insiders can be wrong and mis-time their purchases or sales. Second, insider-trading reports can be quite dated, perhaps being published 30 days or longer after the proposed transaction. In effect such old news would be of less benefit to your current trading expectations. Lastly, insiders will often buy or sell shares for reasons, which have little, or nothing to do with where they feel the share price is going.

To sum up, insider-trading reports can be a good indication to confirm your trading decisions and are always important to be aware of; however, you should not rely on them alone to make any firm buy or sell decisions on a day-to-day basis.

Remember that the company's you are looking to invest in are PUBLIC companies, their past performance is available for all interested investors to read. You want to invest in companies that have performed well in the past with the expectation and increased probability that they will continue to perform well in the future. Try not to be swayed by hot tips, rumors or unexpected news reports. Instead look at the numbers, look at the rate of growth, look at the overall value of the company and base your decision on whether to buy their shares after soberly examining the published facts.

TRADE PUBLICATIONS

A good source of company information can often be found in industry trade publications. These are basically magazines and newsletters that are produced for those within a particular area of expertise. Some examples include: Computer Dealer News, Computing Canada and Info Systems Executive. These are available from Plesman Publications at www.plesman.com. These often give details on company developments that may not make it to the mainstream press. Stories include: new products, new contracts awarded and new strategic alliances within the industry. Subscriptions are free to those qualified in the computer industry and $150 per year for general subscribers.

Other good publications include Ottawa Business Journal and Silicon Valley North published by a division of Newsys Solutions.

You may often receive newsletters in the mail detailing information on penny stocks or small-cap-picks etc. For the most part, these types of publications are biased and unreliable. By examining trade publications you can get real industry news which is much more valuable and accurate. There are good newsletters out there, but you will usually have to pay for them.

To sum up, don't be afraid to roll up your sleeves and do a little digging on the company's you are interested in. Keep your eyes and ears open. You don't need to be a private investigator or a forensic accountant but examining the basics will go a great distance towards helping you make correct investment decisions.

6

New Economy,
New Technology

Be thou diligent to know the state of thy flocks, and look well to thy herds for riches are not forever.

Prov. 27 23-24

There has been a lot of buzz in the press lately about "New Economy" stocks. Often new economy is considered Internet based companies as opposed to traditional "bricks and mortar" businesses. For our purposes let's define new economy as companies whose main business is involved in the following areas: Internet, computers, semiconductors, communications, as well as: satellite, electronics and related industries. Old economy companies would include: resources (mining, forestry etc) banking, retail based and traditional manufacturing (automotive, machinery etc).

It is not difficult to realize that there has been an explosive increase in global communication and commerce since the 1900's. Basically with the advent of the telephone at the turn of the last century, the citizens of the world have begun to interconnect at an exponential rate. It is as if the earth is one giant brain that has been forming and just recently begun to develop the electrical interconnections required to allow productive global thought. While still in it's infancy, it is clear that any technology, which facilitates this global communication, will be in immediate high demand. Faster and more efficient communications are required to promote the distribution of goods and services amongst nations. Mutually beneficial trading relations have always been a positive motivating force behind the advancement of civilized society.

While traditional old economy firms have been able to meet local demand with 10% growth per year, new economy companies have found that they are addressing needs on a much larger scale. They are seeing anywhere from 40% to triple digit annual growth and beyond. Why is this? The earth is racing to envelope itself with a mesh of inter-connections; not only does it facilitate the commerce of old economy companies but the demand exists for the sake of communication itself. The fact that a university professor in Australia wants to get information from a library in Canada is reason enough to contribute to the demand for increased communication ability. The Internet is a very natural and inevitable development of the need for global communication.

Will this demand continue? Absolutely, the global-brain is only seeing the first few flickers of its neurons beginning to hesitantly flicker on and off. The demand for efficient bandwidth and clear connections will promote a diverse latticework of compatible communication solutions. Areas contributing to the demand will include hardware (all types of computer-like devices as well as all types of repeater type hardware i.e. hubs, routers, switches, cables, fiber optics, semiconductors etc.) software, telecommunication (anything phone/voice related) wireless communication (anything based on RF technology) satellite communication, video communication. (Global video inter-communication has yet to even be a blip on the map as far as global development goes). Some of these categories may overlap to some degree and there will be new categories that will develop as well. Remember the statistics about China, with one quarter of the world's population, most of its citizens do not own a telephone–demand is still growing and will continue to grow for the foreseeable future.

Does this mean that any company involved in these industries will prosper? Absolutely not, but the ones that do fill these global technology needs efficiently will experience unprecedented prosperity. Because the growth rates for new technology type companies can be so rapid, the traditional methods of assessing the value of a particular company's shares may be difficult. So much emphasis is placed on future potential that the share price may seem to be way overvalued as well as subject to high levels of volatility.

Here is a list of Technology Firms currently trading on the TSE that are also part of the TSE 300:

Hardware:

ATY—	ATI TECHNOLOGIES INC
BAE—	BAE SYSTEMS CANADA INC.
CMS—	C-MAC INDUSTRIES INC.
CAE—	CAE INC.
CLS—	CELESTICA INC.
CIC—	CERTICOM CORP.
GND—	GENNUM CORP.
JDU—	JDS UNIPHASE
LTV—	LEITCH TECHNOLOGY CORP.
MLT—	MITEL CORP.
MCL—	MOORE CORP.
NII—	NORSAT INTERNATIONAL INC.
NT—	NORTEL NETWORKS CORP.
RND—	RAND TECHNOLOGY CORP.

RIM— RESEARCH IN MOTION LIMITED
SW— SIERRA WIRELESS
TKX— TEKLOGIX INTERNATIONAL INC.
TUN— TUNDRA SEMICONDUCTOR CORP.
WIN— WI-LAN INC.

Software:

BKB— BAKBONE SOFTWARE INC.
IFM— BCE EMERGIS INC.
GIB.A— CGI GROUP INC.
COG— COGNICASE INC.
CSN— COGNOS INC.
COR— COREL CORP.
CRE— CREO PRODUCTS INC.
CRY— CRYPTOLOGIC INC.
DSG— DESCARTES SYSTEMS GROUP INC.
GAC— GEAC COMPUTER CORP.
HUM— HUMMINGBIRD LTD.
MMD— MDSI MOBILE DATA SOLUTIONS INC.
MGI— MGI SOFTWARE CORP.
IFN— NURUN INC.
OTC— OPEN TEXT CORP.
ZIC— ZI CORP.

Telephone Related:

AIT— ALIANT INC.
BCE— BCE INC.
BI— BELL CANADA INTERNATIONAL INC.
CN— CALL-NET ENTERPRISES INC.
NET.A— CLEARNET COMMUNICATIONS INC.
MBT— MANITOBA TELECOM SERVICES INC.
MTI.B— MICROCELL TELECOMMUNICATIONS INC.

RCM.B—ROGERS CANTEL MOBILE COMMUNICATIONS
TGO— TELEGLOBE INC.
TIW— TELESYSTEM INTERNATIONAL WIRELESS INC.
T— TELUS CORP.

Miscellaneous Technology:
SAT— CANADIAN SATELLITE COMMUNICATIONS INC
RCI.B— ROGERS COMMUNICATIONS INC.
BII— BID.COM INTERNATIONAL INC.

This list is by no means exhaustive as it only represents those that are in the TSE300 category. Stocks are selected to be in the TSE300 based on various factors such as market capitalization. It is beneficial for a company to be included in the TSE300 index due to increased exposure and prestige. This can lead to increased investor interest and a corresponding increase in demand for their shares, which of course contributes to a higher share price. It would be valuable to identify companies on the TSE that would fit into the categories listed above but are too small or too new to be eligible. Since the list is always being updated, you must be on the lookout for smaller companies that are growing with the potential to be added to the TSE300 Index and of course avoid those that are being dropped due to negative performance. Many companies will be dropped from the list due to mergers and acquisitions with other publicly traded companies. Some of the best opportunities for public technology companies are during their growth from market capitalization of 200 million to one billion dollars, giving investors a five-fold return on investment.

These four categories, hardware, software, telephone related and miscellaneous technology (expect to see this category expand in the future) are the areas that will likely experience the greatest levels of growth over the next 5-10 year time period. This is the time when you as an investor want to find stocks that will dramatically increase in value.

Personally I don't put quite as much faith in software as I do the other three categories. The reasons for this include: 1) highly competitive environment 2) significant market dominance by Microsoft 3) subject to piracy. These factors can be particularly detrimental to software companies that are targeting the retail consumer market. The business-to-business software market is affected by these factors to a much lesser degree. There are still great opportunities for software companies that are leaders in a specific area of expertise.

Most if not all of the Canadian technology companies listed above are world-class organizations. That is, they can effectively compete and fill demand on a global scale. These are the type of companies you want to partner with as an investor.

7

Buy and Hold—Patience Wins

Better is the end of a thing than the beginning thereof: and the patient in spirit is better than the proud in spirit.

Eccles 7 v8

When I was in my twenties, I spent a lot of time trading futures. I gained a lot of experience in the exciting world of commodities. Pork bellies, coffee, silver, and T-Bonds alike, you name it, I traded it. Trading in these markets involves high levels of leverage, that is to say, your position is margined to the extreme, turning minor moves in the price of a commodity into financial life and death situations. Trading in futures is like trying to leap buck naked over a six foot wall of razor wire; you might survive but you're probably gonna end up in pretty bad shape. Needless to say, I moved a lot of money around trading futures but it did not make me rich.

Fast forward to my to my thirty-something years as a corporate drone, mindlessly enduring life in my Dilbertian cubicle while day-dreaming of umbrella drinks in the Caribbean. I knew there were some real honest to goodness opportunities in the Canadian high technology marketplace but was not willing to analyze the market to death. I had been dabbling in stocks for some time, but never felt they could offer the explosive returns that I had experienced trying to leap over razor wire...that is until I learned to be patient. You see, a trade that you might execute in two or three hours in the futures market could be slowed down and essentially be played out in stocks in two or three weeks. The advantage towards stocks is that you have time to actually look for solid fundamentals rather than rely on speculative seat-of-the-pants trading.

I purchased 2500 of Research in Motion at between $5 and $6 in early 1998 and felt this company had great potential to grow. I had looked at their products, visited their location in Waterloo, contacted their chief financial officer etc. Just basically as much fundamental investigation as possible. Since I was working full time and did not have the leisure to look at stocks from a technical viewpoint, I simply bought the shares and since I was in the black almost right away, just held onto them. Even though I continued to place many other trades, this was one stock that I more or less wanted to hold for the long term. For the beginning investor, this is the best strategy I can recommend; don't worry too much about trying to time the market, simply find a good company and buy and hold.

Take a look at the large cap companies listed in the chapter entitled Current Opportunities and pick one. Then research the small caps and pick one of them. Split your investment 50/50 and buy and hold. When you trading account starts to reach $100,000 you will certainly want to be a little more diversified, but while you are beginning and making regular contributions to your trading account, the buy and hold strategy will serve you well.

Research in Motion noted in their latest annual report that $100 invested in their stock in February 1998 turned into over $2400 by February 2000! That's only two years! Imagine if you invested $10,000 into this stock and saw your investment grow to $240,000 in just two short years. Unfortunately I sold most of my shares at $140 only to see the share price continue up to $260 but with the stock currently trading back under $100, the opportunity for at least doubling or tripling one's investment in a relatively short period is still present with this dynamic and innovative company.

A good way to get motivated about the merits of a buy and hold strategy is to look at the concept of exponential returns. Suppose you invest $10,000 into a company that is steadily growing its revenues at 40% per year. You know that share price is directly related to revenue (as long as they maintain profit margins) so let's assume that the share price matches exactly the revenue growth. (Some companies share price growth will actually surpass their revenue growth as they gain greater exposure to a wider audience of investors). The following chart shows what could happen if you invested $10,000 into a high-growth company:

	PORTFOLIO VALUE	NET ANNUAL GAIN
END OF YEAR 1	$14,000	$4,000
END OF YEAR 2	$19,600	$5,600
END OF YEAR 3	$27,440	$7,840
END OF YEAR 4	$38,416	$10,976
END OF YEAR 5	$53,782	$15,366

Of course not many companies can experience year over year 40% growth; however the point here is to look at the net annual gain column. What do you notice? The investor in the above example is getting a raise every year without putting in any more money! The company maintains a constant growth rate while your net annual gain increases year over year. You are looking directly at one of the reasons why the rich get richer and the poor…well, you know what happens to the poor; they stay poor.

But what about volatility you ask; a lot of Canadian stocks bounce back and forth and end up no different at the end of a few months as they were at the beginning. When using a buy and hold strategy you are not concerning yourself with weekly or monthly fluctuations. Look at stocks like Celestica, JDS and Nortel and you will see the consistent up-trend in share price year over year that you are trying to find. Also don't be afraid to buy and hold small cap companies. If the product demand is strong, a good management team is in place and the shares are fairly valued to start with, it will not be difficult to find stocks that will double and triple in price over the course of a year.

When I kept my investments restricted to fast growing companies and I started to realize the above concept, it dramatically changed the way I looked at wealth creation. If you look at the percentages and work out the math, you will begin to realize how much more efficient it is to be an investor than a salaried employee. When you start to consistently see your net worth increase by thousands of dollars week after week, you know that your days at the office are numbered. It will quickly become inefficient for you to continue working for someone else when you can earn in a month what your job will pay you in a year.

While pretending to work in you cubicle, re-do the table above using an example with a company growing at 10% per year and changing your initial investment to $100,000. Expand the time frame out to 10 years and see what type of annual increase you get. Use a variety of growth rates and time frames and see how long it takes to reach $1 million. Compare the **NET ANNUAL GAIN** from investing in a growing company with the 5% annual kick-in-head pay raise you get from your current photocopy-water cooler position.

If you've ever wondered why people like Warren Buffet and Charlie Munger look so smug, it is because they keep a table like the one above neatly folded in their back pocket and they don't expect you to understand it. What kind of free-market utopia is this that allows someone to get rich by buying and holding good stocks? Just remember that the person that invests in good stocks is investing in an enterprise that is serving people. If you serve people, you WILL be rewarded. Instead of trying to serve people by stapling papers and taking two fifteen-minute breaks per day, think about ways to serve people by investing in companies that are meeting the needs of thousands upon thousands of consumers. If you do, your annual pay raises will far exceed those being meted out in the labor market.

On a more serious note, I don't want the reader to sense that I have no respect for the humble Canadian worker. A part of my ethos as an investor is a belief in Canadian productivity. I am proud of the contributions my co-workers and I were able to make at the companies I was employed with; but I am also keenly aware of the hindrances to effectiveness that exist in corporate culture. In fact being productive to the bottom line is usually the easy part of being in the workplace; it is the required human interactions that drive you up the wall. There are large numbers of highly talented and motivated Canadians in various high-technology areas, and it these people that I hope to continue to support and partner with as I seek out investment opportunities.

Remember that with a buy and hold strategy, your greatest gains will be during the latter part of your investment time horizon. Patience is a must. Investigate and understand the concept of exponential growth.

8

Technical Analysis

*He becometh poor that dealeth with a slack hand, but
the hand of the diligent maketh rich.*

Prov. 10 4

We now come to the most dynamic aspect of investing, which involves
the concept of market timing. Before getting into the ins and outs of
trading let me mention a two-step plan.

For the investor just starting out, certainly the best strategy for
solid gains is to buy and hold. That is, find a solid company that is
experiencing 40% annual growth or greater and invest for the long
term. (Long-term referring to 5+ years time frame.)

As your portfolio starts reaching around the $100,000 threshold, it
starts to become more efficient as well as psychologically more bearable
to have large portion of funds available in cash to be ready for short-
term market opportunities. I do not advocate the idea of day trading,
that is buying and selling stocks over the span of a few minutes or
hours. Unless you really want to be a slave to a computer screen, in an
atmosphere of trying to win at video-poker; I would suggest, rather, a

much more stable and lucrative approach. That is, taking advantage of cyclical stock price fluctuations based on daily technical indicators.

You can access the charted price history of stocks from a number of sites on the Internet. I happen to use the excellent resources of Data Broadcasting Corporation at www.dbc.com.

Take a look at the following chart of price history for OnX Incorporated, ticker symbol ON.

The following chart is very simple to understand. It shows the date on the bottom, volume of shares traded is measured on the lower third portion of the chart and is represented as vertical bars. (The higher the bar, the higher the volume) The upper two thirds, the chart itself, shows the price history by plotting the open, high price, low price, and close. Thus, this type of chart is often called an OHLC chart. The first day of trading for OnX followed the second example below, where the opening price was the low of the day and the closing price was the high of the day.

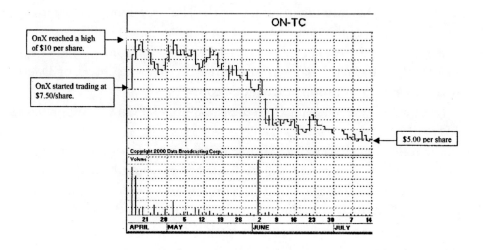

I've excluded the right side price axis for simplicity. OnX is provider of e-business solutions to fortune 1000 companies. They are not part of the TSE 300. They have a market capitalization of about $125 million ($5 share price x $25 million shares outstanding)

Revenues have grown from $108 million in 1998 to $149 million in 1999, growth of almost 40%, their net earnings are positive (about .21 cents per share). Revenue to market capitalization is an important comparison. Here we see market cap below revenue, whereas the same company trading on the NASDAQ could trade at a market cap that is a multiple of revenue. (i.e. with rev at $149 million a Nasdaq listed company in the same industry might trade at 2 to 5 times revenues=market cap of $298-$745 million which would give a share price of $11.92 to $29.80 (This is on the conservative side, take a look at I2 technologies; an e-business solution provider; {Nasdaq: ITWO} which trades at a market cap of 30 times revenues!) Needless to say Canadian Technology companies are often much undervalued when compared to their U.S. counterparts in similar categories. This is also one of the reasons that Canadian technology companies will often experience a nice boost if they get listed on the Nasdaq exchange;

U.S. investors see the bargain aspect of the Canadian company and drive the share price up.

OnX recently IPO'ed at $7.50 per share, quickly rose to $10.50 per share and then drifted down to about $5 per share. I had traded OnX on the first few days of trading for a small profit and then exited to allow the shares to "settle". Right away you know that if they IPO'ed at $7.50 per share you are now looking at a stock that is "on sale", you have a chance to buy at a discount to what the original investors paid. This decreases your downside risk to some degree in so far as you are assuming the company will not be going bankrupt and thus the shares will not be going to $0.00.

A good question to ask concerning any technology company is "Are they serving a global demand?" and "Who are their main clients?" While OnX may be mostly involved with servicing clients in Canada, their services are being directed at companies whose focus is global in scope. Also since a lot of their work is with Internet related ventures, their services have potential global impact.

Another good question to ask is "What are the chance that this company could earn $1 per share in the near future?" I estimated that OnX could possibly earn .50 cents per share within 12 months; with an industry acceptable P/E ratio of 25–50, OnX could potentially trade for $12.50 to $25 within 12 months; again this type of thumbnail estimate reduces your potential downside. Always try to mentally calculate what is the likelihood of the company you are examining going bankrupt thus reducing the shares to zero.

Finally, before investing in OnX, I wanted to actually contact the company since their head office is located in Toronto. It is not a huge deal to make a short phone call to ask a few basic questions. I also physically visited their location to confirm that, yes; it is a real live company. Although I didn't actually meet anyone on my visit, I did see client recommendations in the lobby from large companies such as the Bay and Molson's. This helped to confirm to me that they are meeting the needs of the marketplace. This is a key point, as a small investor shouldn't feel embarrassed about visiting a public company to ask a few questions. As a shareholder you are a part owner of the company. Don't be a nuisance but simply make sure that you are dealing with a genuine enterprise as opposed to a post office box location at a drugstore. Any fundamental information you can find out first hand is extremely valuable to your investment focus.

From the above chart, it is difficult to see any reason to want to purchase shares from a technical perspective. That is, the chart above of the company's price and volume does not give any indication of where the price of the stock may have a tendency to go. We have looked at OnX fundamentally and have found that it a sound company with solid revenues, profits and the likelihood of long term gains but what about in the short term? Are there any technical indications that the share priced may be poised to rise?

Take a look at the following chart from OnX, which shows the same time frame but has indicators added to provide a visual analysis of the recent share price activity.

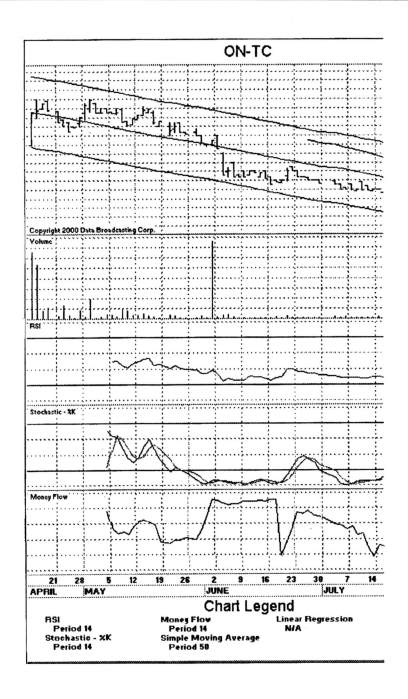

ON-TC

Copyright 2000 Data Broadcasting Corp.

Volume

RSI

Stochastic - %K

Money Flow

| 21 | 28 | 5 | 12 | 19 | 26 | 2 | 9 | 16 | 23 | 30 | 7 | 14 |
| APRIL | | MAY | | | | JUNE | | | | | JULY | |

Chart Legend

RSI	Money Flow	Linear Regression
Period 14	Period 14	N/A
Stochastic - %K	Simple Moving Average	
Period 14	Period 50	

The charting tools available from Data Broadcasting Corp at www.dbc.com are simple to apply. They have the best technical charting tools I have found on the web and they are available to any investor. Check out their web site for yourself and read the technical indicator definitions in the glossary at the back of this book.

You can see in the above chart that we have superimposed a **Linear Regression** indicator over the OHLC (open-high-low-close) chart body (the three downward sloping parallel lines) as well as a moving average line (not enough price history to be significant).

A linear regression superimposed on a daily price chart gives a good envelope of where price activity tends to range. That is, the linear regression corridor gives a good visual on whether a particular stock price is 'relatively' high or low.

We are also looking at the **Relative Strength Index** that measures how often the price of the stock is closing at a higher price than the previous day, reflecting the upward momentum. The relative strength index can give an excellent indicator for taking profits when it breaks above the upper 80% line.

Also plotted on the graph above is **Stochastics** and **Money Flow**. Stochastics gives a measure of relative price digression and money flow gives a measure of relative buying or selling pressure based on the amount of volume on 'up days' versus the amount of volume measure on 'down days'. The stochastic indicator was developed by George C Lane and gives a measure of a stock's price in relation to its recent highs and lows. (See Appendix for detailed definition)

There are dozens of indicators that technical analysts use to try and predict future stock prices. Some are widely known and others are secret calculations labeled as 'proprietary' indicators. An important thing to remember is that all technical indicators measure the past price activity and have no real predictive ability. There may be some very sophisticated indicators that incorporate neural network analyses with Deep Blue running the calculations and so on, but if the company you are looking at gets nuked tomorrow morning, all your technical analysis is out the window.

What technical indicators CAN do for you is give you an indication of what is likely to happen. Is this valuable? Extremely! At the risk of contradicting the previous paragraph, **technical indicators can increase your chance of predicting future price activity because of the fact that price activity moves in waves and follows patterns that occur repeatedly over time**. How often do you see a price chart that 'moves' at right angles over time? The natural flow of price action is a wave. Gradual increase, accelerated interest in the stock and corresponding price, leveling off and then gradual selling and accelerated selling. Said another way, prices in the stock market generally follow a natural ebb and flow. Even sharp spikes and sharp declines can often be foreshadowed by the previous price and volume activity.

With this in mind, it often becomes a matter of personal preference which indicators to follow. For example Peter Lynch uses charts that superimposes 12 months earnings per share on top of share price to find stocks trading far above or below their earnings. (This presents fundamental information in a visual format, sort of a fundamental/technical combination). People perceive things differently and while one investor may see distinct patterns in technical analysis, the next person may see nothing but randomness. It is difficult to distill technical analysis into concrete principles that are always the 'best' way to predict price activity. While I will present the indicators that I use and find helpful, I want to remind the reader that the indictors I use are by no means exhaustive. Please spend some time to research this area yourself and enjoy the process of finding indicators that you find are helpful. Who knows? You may develop your own proprietary system that works 90% of the time!

Lets look at the chart for OnX on July 16th, 2000 once again:

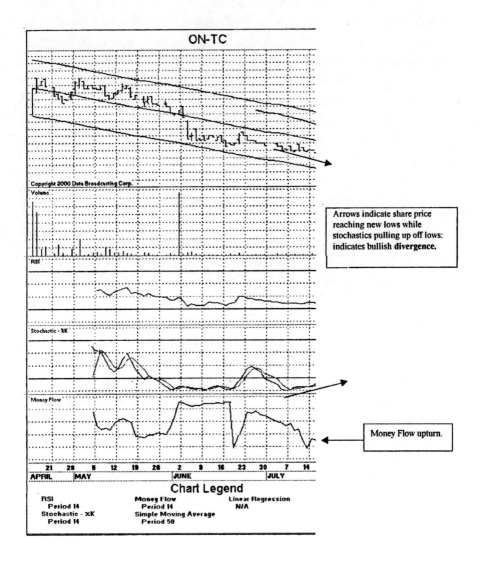

Based on: 1) solid fundamentals 2) stochastic divergence 3) money flow upturn, I purchased 10,000 shares of OnX on July 18th for $4.95 per share.

When a stock price is reaching new lows and the stochastic indicator is moving up off its lows you can see that there is divergence. In the example above, OnX was breaking below $5 per share for the first time while the stochastics were steadily increasing. This has been found to be a strong indicator of a future price increase. Conversely when a stock is reaching new price highs but the stochastic indicator is reaching lower highs, this is often a strong indication of an imminent price drop. By the way, stochastic indicators are calculated using a 'number of days' variable over which the indicator is calculated. I personally use a variable of 14 to 16 days.

WHEN TO SELL?

It is always a good idea to have entry and exit points prior to placing any trade. You want to have a 'target' where you feel the stock price is headed and also a downside price target at which point you will bail out and regroup. Which target is more important? You downside limit! You absolutely must have an exit point at 5%–10% below your purchase price; otherwise your investment capital will be decimated in no time. If you are not willing to take a short term loss, you will never be open to the real huge opportunities that are available to any investor; instead you will get stuck watching 'dogs' that reduce your overall returns but just as importantly tie up your investment capital for too long. Time is the most important factor to consider when trading. How much do you want to make and how long will it take to make? If you are not able to take a loss, you will waste valuable time hoping your stock will turn around. It is like accidentally getting on a bus that is traveling in the opposite direction to where you want to go. You keep hoping that the bus is about to make a u-turn and start getting you to your destination, all the while getting further and further from your destination. You will do much better to get off the bus and start heading in the other direction even if you have to walk!

When using a buy and hold strategy, it is great to be able to hold a stock for a gain of double, triple or the proverbial ten-bagger. (ten times your original investment). In fact for the neophyte investor, I would recommend long term holding of quality technology stocks for exactly those types of returns.

For the short-term trader (holding a stock for a minimum one day to a few months) I recommend the strategy of **Selling Your Investment**. That is, to sell off the number of shares that covers your initial investment. Let's take a look at the trade with Onyx once more:

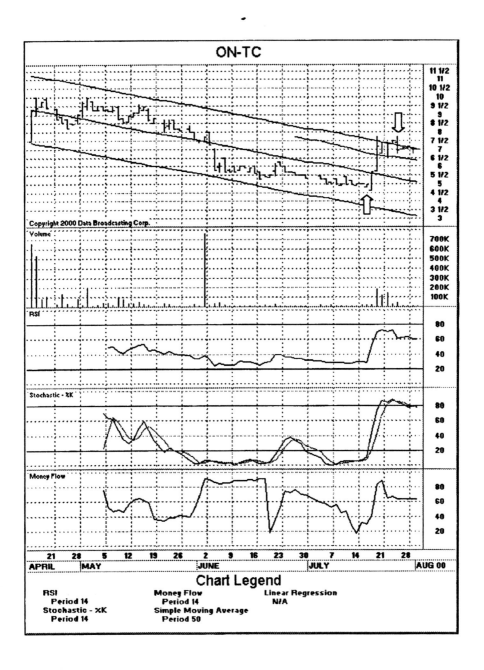

Having bought 10,000 shares at $4.95 on July 18th, I went ahead and sold 7400 shares at $6.75-$6.80 on July 24th, 6 days later, covering my initial investment. I was left with 2600 'free' shares at a value of $18,200. These 2600 shares I can keep on a long-term basis since the fundamentals of OnX remain solid in the foreseeable future. Had I felt OnX to be 'speculative', I would have sold all 10,000 shares for a net gain of $18,000.

Is this trade unusual or difficult? No. I have made trades that were much more profitable and of course some trades that were not as profitable; the reason I detail it here is to show the reader the process and how technical indicators can clarify seemingly random price chart data. Remember, first: fundamental analysis, second: technical analysis and lastly: knowing when to sell.

The beauty of the 'selling your investment' strategy is that it allows you to 1) maintain large cash balances and only place trades when you feel the conditions are right 2) allows the 'fun and excitement' of trading in and out of stocks and 3) it still allows you to participate in a buy and hold strategy with your 'residual shares' i.e. the shares you picked up for free. For example, after the above trade, those 2600 shares of OnX become a permanent buy-and-hold portion of my portfolio. Will I be concerned if the company has a few bad quarters or if the market heads south for the summer? Absolutely not. Those shares remain part of a long-term wealth creation strategy that has survived the test of time and rewarded generations of investors.

Let's look at a chart from Mitel (TSE: MLT):

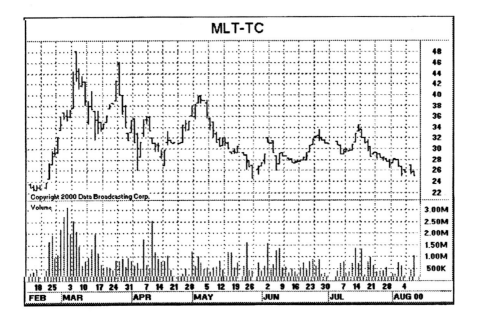

Once again we see a basic price history with little indication of direction or patterns. A buy and hold strategy on this stock from February to August 2000 would have yielded a flat return. Six months is by no means a long time but what about the turmoil of watching you investment achieve huge gains several times and then watching those gains evaporate? Let's add technical indicators for analysis:

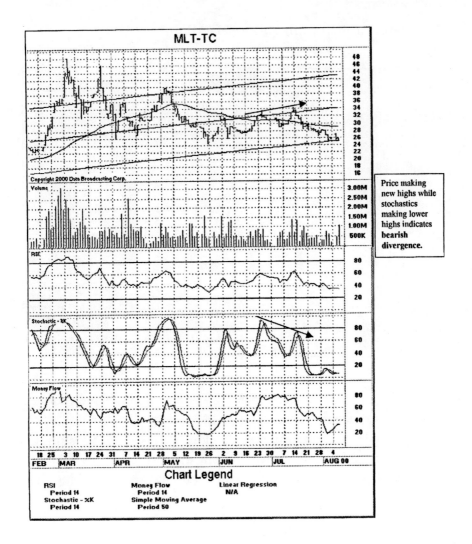

Price making new highs while stochastics making lower highs indicates bearish divergence.

Now you can easily see a strong bearish digression on or about July 14th as the stock price broke $34, a clear signal to take profits and sell.

Try and keep in mind that these chart patterns are not at all rare. They appear and reappear frequently over time. The patient investor merely has to be on the lookout for them.

Let's look at a price history chart for Tundra Semiconductor (TUN):

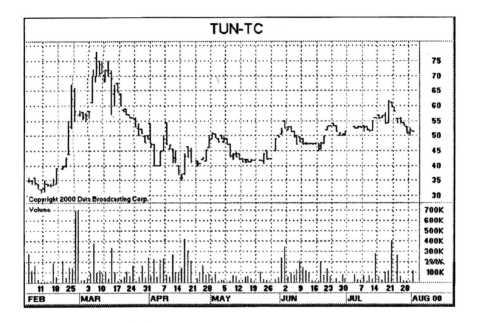

Tundra designs and markets semiconductor chips that perform specialized functions in embedded computer systems. They are indirectly meeting global demand by supplying customers like Nortel, Lucent and Ericsson. Tundra's president Dr. Adam Chowaniec has gone on record stating he expects Tundra to reach 1 billion in revenue by 2008. So far the company has been growing by 40% annually and is indeed on track to reach that goal or at least near it. Currently the company has a market capitalization of about $700 million, which is about 17 X last years revenue of $40 million.

We can compare Tundra to another Canadian Semiconductor company: PMC-Sierra which trades on the Nasdaq under the ticker symbol PMCS. PMC-Sierra has a market capitalization of about $30 billion U.S. which is about 75 X last years revenue of $389 million

U.S. PMC Sierra is farther along the growth cycle as a company with a larger number of employees, larger revenues, greater exposure to U.S. institutional investors etc. However the companies are involved in basically the same general technology space.

If Tundra continues to grow as it has been, it will reach sales of $389 million in about 5 years. What could the market capitalization be at that time? If the market cap to revenue ration remains constant, MC/R=17, we would see a market cap of $6.6 billion cdn. This would translate into a per share price of $470 ($6.6 billion divided by 14 million shares outstanding). Likely the stock would split several times by then.

What if Tundra reached the same level of exposure as PMCS and traded at a market cap to revenue ratio of 75? That would give a market cap of $30 billion cdn and a corresponding share price of over $2000.00! Your $10,000 investment today would translate into $400,000 in 5 years! Impossible? Maybe not, there are of course many factors that would need to be taken into account including, competition, technology changes, economic downturns, etc. There is also the possibility of Tundra issuing more shares to raise cash for expansion, thus diluting the numbers in the above example. The point I am trying to make is that even while being conservative, it is quite likely that Tundra has strong upside potential from its' current $50 share price. This is the type of stock that would be very forgiving if you happen to buy at a relative 'high' point. With a few months of patience, the share price will no doubt continue upwards past your purchase price as the company's revenues increase.

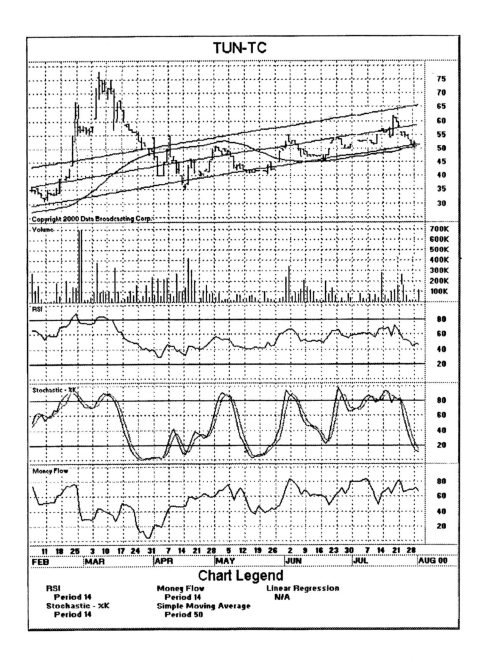

Now we are looking at the same price chart for Tundra with Technical Indicators applied. There is no bullish divergence but it still clear that we are at a 'relative' low. Tundra is trading at the lower lip of the linear regression indicator and the stochastics have dipped below the lower end 20 range. Based on strong fundamental data and satisfactory technical indicators, I went ahead and purchased 2000 shares of Tundra at $50 on July 31st, 2000.

About three weeks later I sold the same 2000 shares at $61.25 on August 23rd. (See chart)

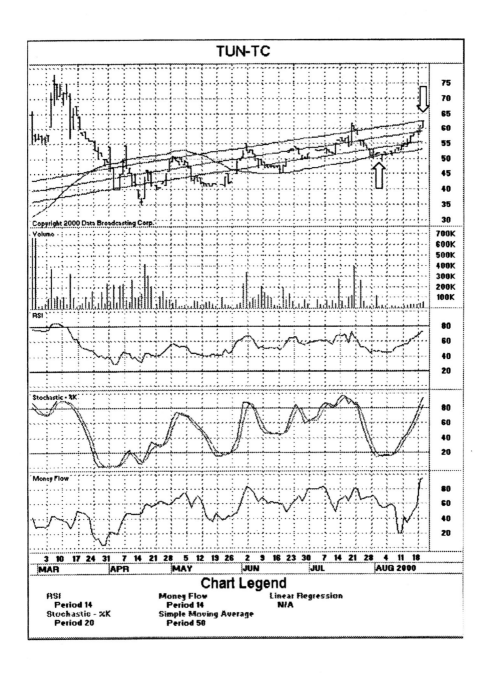

I have indicated the buy and sell points in the preceding chart with arrows. This was the chart I examined from Data Broadcasting Corporations website on the morning of Aug.23rd. This information is available free to anyone with Internet access. You can see how the stochastic indicator has surpassed the upper 80 level indicating a relative high, the money flow indicator has also peaked. The price is also near the upper range of the linear regression channel. All are indications of a good time to take profits.

Commission was $60 to buy and $60 to sell. Net profit on this trade was $22,380. That is over 22% return on investment. To get this type of return in a mutual fund for a year would be outstanding but this was realized after only three weeks! Was this gambling? No, the initial investment was made after a thorough examination of fundamental information. Tundra is a financially sound company with increasing revenue and strong profitability. The technical indicators merely give you a clearer picture of relative price activity. In this particular case, I decided to sell all of 2000 shares. I could have sold 1635 shares to cover my initial investment (1635 x $61.25=$100,143) and been left with 365 'free' shares.

Some people will look at this trade and feel that $22,000 is not much of a return but the actual dollar value is not important, it is the mechanics of the trade that I want to emphasize. There is nothing limiting the reader from buying more shares. Others may look at this trade and feel overwhelmed; they cannot imagine investing so much money at one time. Again, don't look at the actual size of the trade. The same decisions can be made using 10 shares, 100 or 10,000; you have to start somewhere. Also consider that I started trading with what I had. I was in debt with negative net worth and began trading with $15,000 of borrowed money. Hopefully the reader will have a better start than myself but it is never too late to start. Never tell yourself that you can't because of your difficult financial situation.

One does not have to be in a rush to find investment opportunities. They are there now and most likely will still be there next month or next year. For this trade with Tundra, there was never a feeling of urgency; once the opportunity presents itself, the decision to buy or sell can be made confidently without trying to squeeze every penny out of a trade. I often place my trades as 'market orders'–that is I accept the ask price when buying and I accept the bid price when selling. It is better to be more concerned about getting your order filled properly than losing a fraction of a dollar on the share price.

Edwin Lefévre in the classic book, Reminiscences of a Stock Operator, wrote: " I cannot help but make money, I always buy too late and sell too soon!" What did he mean by this? He meant that he bought shares after an up-trend had already been established and sold before the stock was peaking in a buying frenzy. So remember this phrase to help you from trying to be too precise in your buying and selling-or from trying too hard to get all the available profit. Trying to buy at the absolute low and sell at the absolute apex is essentially an exercise in futility.

I decided that the overall market at this time was at a relative high so I chose to sell all 2000 shares. The following chart shows the TSE300 at the time of selling my shares in Tundra.

You can see that there is a slight bearish divergence between the TSE300 level and the stochastic indicator. Also the index is trading at the upper range of the linear regression channel and is significantly above its' 50 day moving average line.

When the price (value) of an index is trading significantly above its long-term moving average, logic suggests it cannot maintain that level indefinitely. An average by definition shows a level that is relatively normal. Deviations from the norm will be short lived with activity alternatively trading above and below the average over time. It is good when using technical analysis to think in terms of what is **likely** or **probable.** You don't have to rack your brain to try and pinpoint exact turning points; it is enough to get a visual image to help you determine a relative range, a best guess so to speak. **Buy on fundamentals; sell on technicals** can be a reliable axiom for a short-term trader. The better-known phrase amongst investors is to buy on rumor and sell on fact (news). (That is, prices of stocks often rise when there are rumors swirling about a company and as soon the news is released to the public, the share price drops as investors scramble to take profits.)

The reader may be wondering if technical indicators seem to be useful when looking at daily charts, why not use them for intra-day trading on an hourly basis? From my past experience I would not recommend this due to two main reasons. One is that the bid and ask spread on a lot of Canadian companies is quite significant, making it difficult to buy and sell quickly and to your benefit. And secondly, intra-day indicators may be using fewer amounts of data resulting in wild swings in the indicator, which in turn can give false buy and sell signals.

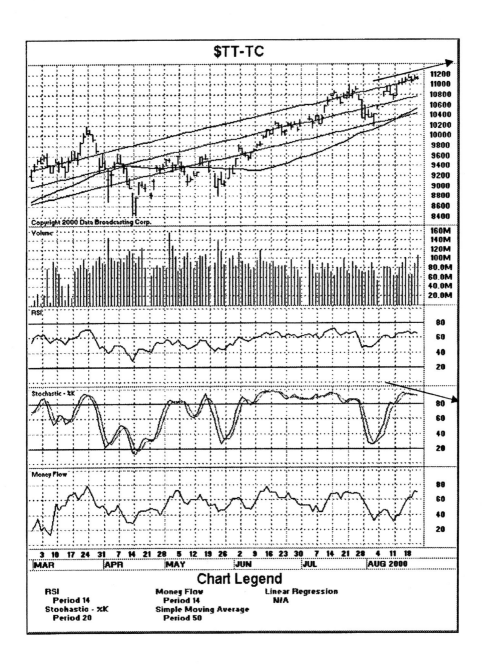

$TT-TC

Copyright 2000 Data Broadcasting Corp.

Volume

RSI

Stochastic - %K

Money Flow

| MAR | APR | MAY | JUN | JUL | AUG 2000 |

Chart Legend

RSI	Money Flow	Linear Regression
Period 14	Period 14	N/A
Stochastic - %K	Simple Moving Average	
Period 20	Period 50	

Preceding chart shows TSE300 index when taking profits on Tundra Semiconductor.

Let look at another example; Eiger Technology is a Canadian Technology company with interests in Stratford, Ontario, South Korea, New Jersey and California. Eiger manufactures MP3 players, fax/modems and ADSL modems, (a new modem standard that still uses copper phone lines, but delivers data about 20 times faster than a 56k modem). Again examine the plain price history chart first:

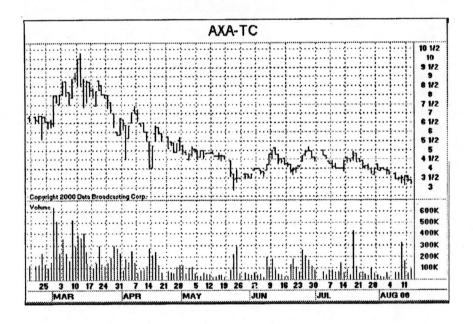

Nothing from the above chart indicates a clear reason to buy. However some technical analysts might notice a 'double bottom' formation. The price of the stock hit a low of about $3 in late May, rose a bit, and then dipped to the $3 level again in mid-August. Fundamentally Eiger has been experiencing stunning growth, recently announcing year over year growth of over 400%. The president has gone on record as saying that he expects revenue growth to continue at that rate for the next six months and also for next year.

The first question I always ask is, " Are they addressing global demand?" For Eiger, the answer is yes; they are supplying oem's (original equipment manufacturers) with MP3 players and modems. Their clients include Samsung and Lucent. I found information in a trade publication (Computer Dealer News) that indicated that Eiger is experiencing tremendous growth and is planning to market under their own brand name, (perhaps an opportunity for increased margins).

Their latest financial results indicated a one-time charge of 1.6 million for re-locating a production facility; thus temporarily understating profitability. They have $10 million in cash and nominal debt. Market cap is $90 million and revenue for latest 12-month period is about $45 million giving a MC/R ratio of 2. If revenues increase to $200 million as predicted, market capitalization should potentially increase as well. If MC/R ratio remained constant his would put share price at over $13 per share. Likely MC/R would drop unless exposure for the company increased, which could be achieved by a NASDAQ listing. Again you should ask yourself, what is a company that is producing revenues of $45 million worth? How profitable are they? What would you be willing to buy the company outright for? By asking these questions and examining companies in the same industry, you will get a feel of whether the company is fairly valued or not. Now let's look at the technical indicators on Eiger.

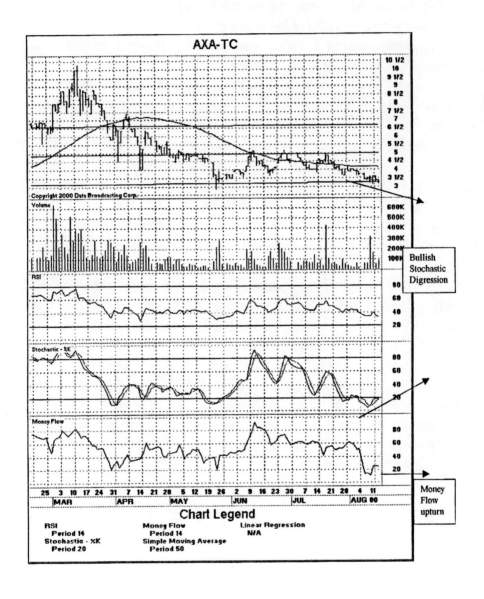

Here we see that Eiger is trading at the low end of its linear regression channel. It is also below its 50-day moving average and we have a bullish stochastic digression along with a money flow upturn. Since we have positive fundamentals and positive technical indicators, I went ahead and purchased 10,000 shares at $3.35 per share on Aug 16th, 2000.

Next is a price chart on Eiger from September 1st where I sold 8500 shares at $3.95 covering my initial investment and leaving me 1500 'free' shares worth over $5,000. This amounts to over 14% return in two weeks.

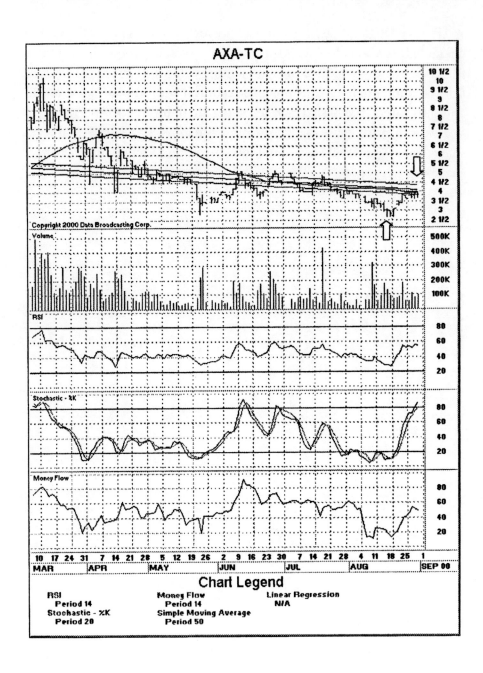

It is important to remember that this charting information is available FREE off the internet. These technical indicators don't have any special predictive power. They are merely giving the investor a clearer visualization of the natural ebb and flow of the marketplace.

Try and put the previous trade into perspective. I invested $33,500 for a period of two weeks. At the end of two weeks, I received back my initial investment of $33,500 so I was only exposed to market risk for those 15 days. I am left with 1500 shares valued at $5,925 that I can sell at any time or hold for long term appreciation. Can you see the potential, efficiency and low risk of this? I could have put $33,500 into an equity mutual fund for 12 months and have no guarantee of a positive return. You have to ask what is riskier, making your own buy and sell decisions or handing money over to total strangers who are charging a fee and delivering, in most cases, less than spectacular returns. The answer should be clear.

Could I have lost money on this trade? Absolutely. Was it risky? Yes, there will always be risk involved but that is why you examine the fundamentals. To make an informed, calculated risk is often not all that risky after all. To let someone else handle your money for you while making you feel secure can be very risky.

The most difficult aspects of executing trades like the ones above are probably the psychological factors that are involved in trading successfully. Which brings us to our next chapter.

9

Do You Believe?

For as he thinketh in his heart, so is he.

Prov 23 7

Stock prices embody a distillation of all the market participants hopes and fears at any given time so it is no surprise that market psychology and hence individual trader beliefs are so important to being successful in the buying and selling of stocks.

My sincere hope is that this book falls into the hands of as many 18-25 year olds as possible. It is generally the young who have not had their faith surgically removed by the operations of life. These are the ones who actually believe that they have the ability to employ the wondrous workings of cause and effect to their own personal benefit. That is, they believe that they CAN get ahead and succeed.

Many people over the age of thirty are severely limited by learned helplessness. These are the masses of people who, should they happen to actually have a few extra thousand dollars to invest, take these dollars and give them to someone they don't know that well, who in turn mis-manages their money and charges them a fee for doing so! These strangers ("investment experts" and mutual fund managers for example) charge their fee off the top, they over-diversify to guarantee mediocre returns and finally provide infrequent and ambiguous reports on their own performance. The only people laughing harder than Canadian mutual fund managers are Canadian bankers.

Canadians spend thousands of dollars in credit card interest every year but probably don't know how to borrow to invest. They don't know the difference between good debt and bad debt. Some will gladly put out hard earned cash for lottery tickets, sports pools at work or even casinos but would never "play" the stock market because it is too risky.

If you want to talk risk let me tell you about an interesting phenomenon. How often have you seen someone risking his or her life to catch a bus? I see it in Toronto all the time. It is probably safe to assume that the majority of people who take public transit are not financially independent but to see their capacity for risk, they should be millionaires several times over. Why will people run against a red light, stop traffic and nearly kill themselves to catch a bus when there will be another in 15 minutes anyway. Is being late for work worth dying for? These same people who risk life and limb on the street would probably balk at the idea of investing $1000 on a favorite stock. The worst I can lose on any given trade is about $3000–$5000 from the comfort of my home. The real risk-takers are in the streets of Toronto trying to catch buses.

You can only succeed in investing in stocks if you BELIEVE you can. It does take some work, it also takes some time but the benefits far outweigh the sacrifice in time and effort. If you think making your own stock choices is too risky then you probably have never tried. Or you have tried and then ran into too many mistakes. If you invest for yourself, you WILL make mistakes, you WILL have losing trades; but to make sure that your winners outweigh your losers is not all that difficult. Stocks that go up tend to keep going up just like companies that grow 30% one-year will likely grow the next. Anyone will succeed if they hold their stocks that rise and sell their stocks that fall. Unfortunately people do not have the discipline to follow this simple strategy. They do not have the discipline because they have been conditioned to believe that they should fail. This belief has been so firmly entrenched that they subconsciously sabotage their own simple success. This is why it so easy to hold a losing stock for months and months and why it is so painful to hold onto a stock that is increasing in value by leaps and bounds. For those with investment experience, the above scenario is all too painfully familiar but probably sounds quite odd to the 18 year old who has never traded a stock in his or her life.

Let me tell you a story. There were two men who had gardens. In these gardens, the men planted a variety of seeds. As they watched, day-by-day the plants began to grow. At first all the plants appeared the same, rising through the soil as tender green shoots. After a week of growth it became clear that some of the plants were weeds and some of the plants were nice flowers. Upon noticing the weeds the first man immediately plucked out the weeds from the garden. The second man wasn't quite sure that they were weeds and decided to wait a few days to make sure. After a few more days, the weeds were noticeably larger but he still wanted to wait in case they might actually be flowers when fully grown. At the end of several months, the first man had a garden full of nice flowers; the second man had a garden overgrown with weeds. The second man was still unwilling to remove the weeds since by now they were full of thorns and he thought he might hurt himself by trying to pull them out.

What can we learn from this story? How soon do you dump a stock after it starts to go down? **As soon as you identify it is a weed!** After purchasing a stock, you cannot lie to yourself; there is no room for hoping, wishing or crossing your fingers. You will know in your mind when a stock is a loser, your conscience will tell you. If the stock drops by 5%-10% from your purchase price, get out. But you may say, "What about the buy and hold strategy?" Yes, you are buying and holding for gains not losses. Take a look at your current portfolio and ask yourself what do you see? Weeds or flowers? Most investors have a bunch of small flowers with one huge weed strangling everything. You must be proud of each and every holding in your portfolio at any given time; if not, then what is that stock doing in your portfolio? Get rid of it! Not only do weeds negate the gains of your flowers but also they stifle you from being able to do anything dynamic. Once you rip a major weed out of your portfolio, the psychological relief is often enough to enable you to quickly recoup your loss by investing in a real winning stock. Take the loss, regroup and start getting gains again.

My sister recently showed me an article from the July 2000 issue of a popular woman's magazine. It was a question and answer section on the topic of jobs and money. The question (presumably from a reader) was: " I've finally saved up $2,000 to play with on the stock market. What should I do?" A well-meaning author provided the answer; the first step was to head to a broker and then to invest in a stock mutual fund. To quote: "the broker simplifies the process by doing the paperwork and keeping track of investments for you". To put it bluntly, I would argue that this is bad advice. A broker will complicate the process and probably not keep track of your investments all that well.

To continue with our garden analogy; if you got a broker to help you plant your garden, he or she would drop by your house and take your seeds out of your hands. First he would stuff a portion of the seeds in his pocket for an administration fee. Next he would throw the rest of the seeds in your garden and if he was placing them in a mutual fund, he would wrap the seeds in a plastic bag first. Then he would instruct you not to do anything and call you in a few months if you had any concerns. When you did call, alarmed that nothing is growing, he would chastise you for being too shortsighted and tell you to stay the course. After all, his company is a hundred years old and has gazillions of dollars under management. A year later he would bring you a small plant as a gift and maybe an account statement if you were lucky.

Isn't there a place for brokers in the stock market? Yes, there is lots of work for brokers dealing with large manicured gardens. If you employ a full time gardener then you could probably use a broker. If you employ a full time gardener, you don't need to be reading this book; for everyone else there are some things that are better accomplished firsthand and gardening is one of them.

Let's try another analogy. The stock market is like the ocean; it is cold, unfeeling and dangerous. It is not out to get you; it is just there, like a part of nature. If somebody drops you into the middle of the ocean, you will quickly drown. If you have a life preserver you will last a little longer but will still die. If a freighter picks you up, you can safely cross the ocean. Getting a life preserver is like reading a few books about personal finance. Catching a freighter is when you buy a whack of stock for $5 and sell it 24 months later for $200. Your ideal scenario with respect to survivability would be if the ocean were your natural habitat. Let's say that you are a shark that swims in the ocean. You go where you want, you feed when you want and you breathe the water as naturally as humans breathe air. A shark buys a stock and sells for a profit as naturally as eating. It does not make him elated or giddy when the stock he just bought goes up. Instead he just feels comfortably full after taking a solid profit. If he accidentally chomps down on a bad stock, he spits it out after a few chews and moves on. On the outside the shark may appear aggressive but he is merely purposeful, quiet and focused. Don't confuse the noble shark with the stock promoter, the killer whale of the ocean. Sadistically bloodthirsty, the killer whale kills for the sake of killing. This is why you want to stay away from penny stocks. Penny stocks are the reefs where killer whales roam.

I am not sure if either of these analogies will be helpful for you. The main point to remember is that you must not be intimidated, afraid or feel hopeless about the stock market. When you start a new job and you get a pay-stub with a bunch of different numbers on it, do you take one look at it and then throw up your hands and say, "Oh, I can never understand all these numbers." No, you get someone to explain to you what the deductions mean. If you can understand a pay-stub, you can understand stocks.

Speaking of pay-stubs, if you are still participating in the voluntary drone market (workforce) make sure that your pay is being docked each week with deductions that are going into a stock-savings account. $150 every two weeks gives you $3900 at the end of the year. Two years zips by fast and now you have $7,800 to invest. $7,800 invested in Nortel Networks[3] two years ago (1998) would be worth over-$140, 000 today! (2000)[That's not a typo: $7,800 to $140,000 in two years] So while working at your current job, you could have gone from zero savings to $140,000 in wealth producing assets in four years by having $150 deducted off your pay every two weeks. How much has your net worth actually increased over the last four years?

Maybe you have been regularly contributing $50 a week into mutual funds or your company pension fund. That's a start for sure, but isn't it time to put the pedal to the metal and get things moving? We are living in a dynamic age, which requires dynamic action to take advantage of the opportunities before us. Imagine being able to tell your children or grandchildren that you invested in stocks at the turn of the century. First of all, your inheritance to them will probably be in the millions as opposed to having a meager pension enough to take care of only your-self. Secondly you will be much better positioned to instill in them the confidence they will need to be financially responsible.

And so what if the market crashes and your investments fall. Let's say the market crashes eight years from now, wiping out 90% of your port-folio. 10% of a million is still better than 10% of nothing. Once you

---

3. Nortel is a birthright heritage for Canadians; it is your undeserved reward for being born into the country that invented the telephone. You may as well put 10% of your portfolio into Nortel stock to fulfill your patriotic obligations and then move on to more interesting investments.

reach one million in assets, a large portion of your funds would actually be moved to fixed income investments like bonds and treasury bills so a market crash would likely only affect the small stock portion of your portfolio anyway. Don't procrastinate; there are no solid reasons for NOT being on an aggressive saving and investing plan.

10

Danger

The slothful man saith, there is a lion without, I shall be slain in the streets.

Prov. 22 13

What did the writer mean when he wrote the above quote? The slothful (lazy) man says: " I can't go out there, are you crazy, I'll get killed!" Things have not changed much in 2000 years. People are saying the same thing today. "I can't invest in stocks, are you crazy? I'll get killed!" Fear and laziness keeps people from ever trying. For many people, the "lion" is a stock market crash.

There will always be the doom and gloom type of characters who are constantly predicting a meltdown of the economy into another worldwide depression. These types of people will never be open to opportunities that involve any amount of risk so they are not the people I want to address this book to. Rather I want to reach those average readers who may be wary and are simply trying to avoid unnecessary risk. I want to encourage people in this category that trying to avoid a market crash is an exercise in futility. Beyond maintaining a healthy portion of one's portfolio in cash, there will always be the danger of market corrections. This should be looked at as the price of admission to stock market profits. Not everyone can stomach the idea of share price volatility. The stock investor can take pride in the fact that they have membership in an elite group of strong-willed individuals. These are the ones that are willing to risk their cash for the chance of financial reward.

We cannot deny that real danger exists in the world of investing. But where do these dangers lie? Is the danger in the market itself or can we look at the investor. A lot of the danger can be found by looking at the individual that loses money. The danger of overconfidence, the danger of greed and the danger of unfounded assumptions are all very serious. These dangers are actually more insidious than bad stocks. A bad stock can always be sold but the dangers of overconfidence, greed and assumption stay with a person and affect all the decisions he or she makes on each and every trade.

You can see these traits in evidence when someone is losing money in a bull market. In their haste to grab every cent, they buy and sell haphazardly like a dog trying to catch his tail. That is greed in action. You can see assumption when someone buys a penny stock based on a new technological breakthrough story and you can see overconfidence fade to anguish as their investment is cut in half slowly, painfully and depressingly.

I just read a story of a 41 year-old man that wanted to retire early. He just sold off his business and had $452,000 in cash. Here's the rest of the story as told by Fortune magazine:

> Then he got to thinking. With all that money, why not put a little in the stock market? All his friends were doing it. Why not give it a try? One day in January, he went to see an old buddy who worked at a local bank. "I'm thinking about buying a few stocks," Lavoro told him. "What should I do?" His friend replied, "I have a broker for you." Before he knew it, Lavoro

was on the phone with Richard Berland, a stockbroker for GBI Capital Partners.

It was a milestone for Lavoro. He had never bought a stock. Lavoro made his first foray into the market that very day, buying two small-company stocks. Over the next few weeks, he put more than $200,000 into the account and spoke with Berland daily, experiencing the thrill of investing in a gravity-defying market. He still remembers the day his broker delivered the ultimate rush: His account was up nearly $200,000 in less than a month.

Then his broker told him he could juice his returns by investing on margin–that is, borrowing some of the purchase price of the stocks he was buying. Sure, said the neophyte investor, paying scant attention to the details.

Those details would come back to haunt him. In late February he received a letter instructing him to put $128,000 into his account to cover margin loans. Lavoro was shocked. He didn't realize he says now, precisely what margin was. When the Nasdaq plunged in April, Lavoro was wiped out. He lost his entire savings-$452,000. (GBI says Lavoro was fully aware that he had opened a margin account and that the idea was his.)

Lavoro is only one of countless people who have succumbed to the lure of margin. Certainly, it's not a new phenomenon-its use has long been blamed for contributing to the Crash of '29. But thanks to the stock market's decade-long bull run, qualms about margin have come to seem quaint and old-fashioned.

It's easy to see the allure. Say you want to buy $20,000 worth of stock. With margin, you can borrow $10,000 from your broker to match your initial $10,000 investment. If the company's shares go up 50%, your account grows to $30,000. Once you pay back the loan (plus 7% to 10% interest), you're left with roughly $10,000 in gains-twice as much as you would've had without margin. But just as margin magnifies gains, it also amplifies losses. Say the stock dropped 50%. Now your $20,000 investment is worth only $10,000. Paying off the loan leaves you with nothing, and you're still on the hook for the interest. Your loss on your initial investment is now greater than 100%. If you hadn't borrowed anything, you would've been left with $5,000.

One of the most insidious aspects of margin is that it can force you to lock in your losses. Brokerages typically require that you maintain equity (the current value of your portfolio, minus your margin loan) that is at least 25% of the new market value of that account. If your portfolio falls below that point, you're likely to get the dreaded "margin call": Your broker will demand that you make additional deposits, typically within three days. If you can't or won't, he'll sell your stocks just when you least want him to–when they're falling.[4]

Needless to say, Canadians investors should be on their guard against the above scenario. It is one thing to suffer a painful loss, it is quite another to have one's life savings wiped out. The above series of events should not have to happen to anybody but it will continue to happen as long as there are greedy investors, aggressive brokers and an insatiable marketplace where they can play.

As far dangers inherent in the market itself, there ARE a lot of so-called 'bad' companies to invest in. There IS a lot of misrepresentation that occurs. So how can you protect yourself? Are there common

---

4. Margaret Boitano, FORTUNE, © 2000 Time Inc. All rights reserved.

warning signals that you can look out for? Here are some points you may want to remember:

1) Avoid companies that put more emphasis on attracting new investors to their stock than attracting new employees.

2) Check how many employees a company has. Often companies experience explosive growth after reaching the 100-employee barrier. Some companies that appear huge have only a few employees; often a danger signal.

3) Don't be impressed by companies that appoint status-type directors. For example, a company may appoint an ex-premier to their board to help add credibility in selling shares to the investment community

4) Don't trade on margin. As we saw from the above example, trading on margin is an indication of excessive greed. There is lot's of time to make more money than you will ever need. Slow and steady wins the race.

5) If possible, visit the company you are interested in investing in. Is it a 500 square foot office in an average building of the city's financial district?—Danger. Is it a 50,000 square foot office building in an industrial park with 200,000 square feet of warehouse attached?— Much better. Always ask "How is this company able to serve people?"

6) Read the prospectus on new issues. If not available off the company's website, ask them to mail you one. Read the "risk factors" that are listed in the prospectus.

7) Look at the type of financing the company has negotiated. Especially warrants: what is the exercise price of the warrants, when do they expire? Look at insider sales reports. Is the upper management unloading their shares?

8) Never and I mean NEVER buy shares offered to you over the phone. This one is basic but still needs to be mentioned for the beginner investor. (See glossary on boiler room operation)

9) As in the above example, don't always listen to a broker's recommendations. They are human and just as fallible as you are.

10) Try to avoid trading based on earnings release dates. Stock prices will be volatile at these times; often plummeting as soon as earnings are released even if they are strong results.

Danger will always be present in the stock market, your job as an investor is nullify its' effect by doing your homework and taking control of your decision making behavior.

11

Diligence

The thoughts of the diligent tend only to plenteousness,
but of every one that is hasty only to want.

Prov. 21v 5

Your goal is to be a diligent investor. A diligent investor invests in diligent companies. A hasty investor will try to make a quick buck by investing in penny stocks. A hasty investor responds to 'hot tips'. A diligent investor carefully plans out his or her trades. A hasty investor trades based on emotion and breaking news. A diligent investor trades based on their own research. Make sure that you are a diligent investor.

Diligence according to the dictionary is marked by persevering, painstaking effort. I never looked at it that way actually. But now that I think about it, to be diligent very often requires me to persevere and it usually is a pain to do so. I guess I can agree with that definition after all.

To persevere is defined as: To persist in or remain constant to a purpose, an idea, or a task in the face of obstacles or discouragement. Are you willing to persevere in your investing efforts to hopefully emerge as successful? It will be discouraging at times. When the stock that you told all your friends about starts to tank-that is discouraging. When you buy high and sell low–that is discouraging. When you know the right thing to do and can't seem to do it–that is discouraging. You will no doubt face discouragement and obstacles, but will you persevere?

If making money in stocks were easy, everyone would be doing it right? Wrong. If flying a 747 were easy would everybody be doing it? No, not everyone WANTS to fly a 747. Making money in stocks IS easy once you get the hang of it; it is the difficulties that one encounters or even the difficulties that one hears about that prevents people from attempting to make money or giving up too soon. Remember the analogy of the airline pilot. Do you think the pilot of a 747 considers it difficult to fly the plane? No, in fact he or she probably enjoys it. But ask him or her if it is difficult when they get stuck in a storm, then it is difficult. The successful investor enjoys trading stocks but not when he gets stuck in a sudden market correction.

What can help a person to persevere? That is, what can influence a person to never give up? A good contributor to perseverance is to know that you cannot fail. You will have small failures along the way, but the overall strategy of saving and investing wisely cannot fail. The only barrier to your success is time. As long as you continue to **work, save and invest** you WILL eventually achieve prosperity.

A key exercise in diligence is consistently having deductions taken off your pay and directly transferred into your investment account. This is where you can really put yourself on autopilot towards financial success. If you have $150 taken off your pay every two weeks, that's $3900 per year. Don't worry too much about participating in your companies sponsored plan where they match your contributions to a pension to some degree. Often these types of plans will have restrictions that prevent you from touching the employer-donated portion until you are 65; and even then, the funds may be forced into an annuity. If there are restrictions on your own contributions, do not have anything to do with the plan. Instead set up your own plan with your bank manager.

This practice is vitally important for anyone fresh out of school, all the way up to your 30's and beyond. You must start saving somewhere. Remember the words to the song 'Time' by Pink Floyd?

> Ticking away the moments that make up a dull day
> You fritter and waste the hours in an off hand way
> Kicking around on a piece of ground in your home town
> Waiting for someone or something to show you the way
>
> Tired of lying in the sunshine staying home to watch the rain
> You are young and life is long and there is time to kill today
> And then the one day you find ten years have got behind you
> No one told you when to run, you missed the starting gun[5]

Being diligent is being on a savings plan. Don't just have your savings funneled into an interest bearing passbook account or into a low-return mutual fund. Once you reach $1000 in savings, (after about 3 ½ months of saving) you should be ready to purchase shares in a company that you have been researching. The reader may say, "I cannot afford to save $150 every two weeks". My response to that is simply this; MAKE a way to save, get serious. This is Canada; there is money in the streets. Don't allow any excuses. You have car payments, then sell your car and take the bus. You have to pay rent, then take in a roommate. You have a $1000/month bachelor apartment, then get rid of it and rent a room for $700. There's your $300 of savings per month. The point is: make it happen. Short-term pain for long-term gain. Put your first $1000 of saving into stocks and keep your second $1000 in cash, voila, your portfolio is diversified.

---

5. Pink Floyd, (Mason, Waters, Wright, Gilmour)

Don't whine about not being able to save or not having enough money. Remember that basically everyone has a **marginal propensity to consume** of 1.10. What does that mean? It means that for every extra dollar of earned income you receive, you have a tendency to spend an extra dollar and ten cents. All Canadians have the same marginal propensity to consume. The guy pumping gas at the corner says, "You know I have so many expenses I just don't have any cash to spend. After rent, food and utilities, my paycheck is spent before I get it." The gal that just landed the new Director of Marketing position says, " You know I have so many expenses I just don't have any cash to spend. After the mortgage, food and utilities, my paycheck is spent before I get it." The guy at the gas bar is making $25,000 per year and the Director of Marketing gal is making $75,000 per year. Get the picture. Make your $150 investment savings account deduction your first expense. Get it deducted at the source and put it straight into your self-direct RRSP account as soon as possible so you won't be inclined to touch it. And then one day you find ten years have passed, you either have followed this plan resulting in $100,000 plus in your investment savings account or you are still whining about the bills. It's not gonna happen unless you make it happen.

Finally, diligence means to persevere in learning. Remember what was mentioned in the Foreword about being willing to learn. You must study the basics and teach yourself what works and what doesn't. As your knowledge and experience grows, making money becomes a natural way of living, which helps yourself and those around you.

12

Diversification

Cast thy bread upon the waters: for thou shalt find it after many days. Give a portion to seven and also to eight; for thou knowest not what evil shall be upon the earth.

Eccles.11 1-2

Diversification is dividing up your investment so that all your eggs are not in one basket. Solomon recommended a diversification strategy of seven or eight investments. I agree with this strategy as far actual number of stocks at any one time. Once you start to own more than ten stocks, they may start to get a little more difficult to track and you may start to actually over diversify; a case where your returns drop towards the overall performance of the market indexes. Peter Lynch recommends having as few as five companies in your portfolio at any given time.[6]

Beyond having a variety of stocks in your portfolio I would advocate the concept of using 50% of your invested cash to 'target' a specific

---

6. Peter Lynch, Beating the Street, Simon & Schuster 1994

opportunity while leaving the balance of your invested cash spread out. A sample portfolio might look like the following:

Cash	10%
Nortel Networks	10%
JDS Uniphase	10%
Celestica	10%
C-MAC	5%
RIM	5%
Cash or 'Target Stock'	50%

Your Target Stock would be a short-term trade (one day to 3 months) where you are betting big when the odds are in your favor. In other words, it is a situation where after you have found that the fundamentals of a company are good and you see that the technical indicators are indicating an imminent price increase. In essence you could be keeping as much as 60% of your stock portfolio in cash to be ready for short term opportunities.

This strategy could have you 90% invested in technology stocks at certain times and 40% when not holding a target stock. This may be a little extreme for some people's tastes and I can hear all the certified financial persons calling me crazy and not being diversified at all! I am writing to tell the reader what worked for me and what I believe will continue to work for the foreseeable future. (5+ years) That is not to say I am not open to modifying this strategy. I recently bought and sold shares in Patheon (TSE:PTI) for profit after examining fundamental and technical information on this company (involved in the pharmaceutical industry).

I try and keep my eyes open to other opportunities besides technology but am decidedly biased due to my background in the computer industry. I leave it to the reader to study companies that are experiencing growth that they can understand. If the reader works in a genetic research lab, study the best companies in that area. If the reader is involved in the oil industry or trucking, perhaps they can find successful companies in those areas. With that said, please accept the disclaimer that my diversification is greatly supported by being mostly in cash most of the time. Each beginning investor will quickly get a feel for how to divide up their investments on their own. Use a strategy that you are comfortable with and that allows you to sleep at night.

As your portfolio grows you will want to increase your level of diversification. You can start to put some cash into dividend producing utilities. Trans Canada Pipelines (TSE:TRP) is currently yielding a dividend return of 5.61% with the possibility of capital gain as well. Trans Alta Corp (TSE:TA) is yielding 5.76%. I recently purchased TRP when it was out of favor for $10 per share. At that time the dividend of .80 cents per share was giving a yield of 8% return on investment. That is a very low-risk, decent-return opportunity. You could also purchase some short-term Treasury Bills giving a yield of about 4.75% (30-days).

By starting strong and aggressive with your stock investments, diversification will usually be a natural progression. Don't start your investing efforts by locking your money into a 5-year GIC or buying Canada Savings Bonds that are offered from your friendly neighborhood Human Resources department. You may as well bury your money in the backyard. Make some real investments first and then you can switch to safe, income producing investments after your portfolio has grown.

Every investor will have their own level of risk tolerance and will have to decide on their own how to start. Most investors will reduce their opportunity for profit by stating,

"I just don't have time to sit and watch stocks all day so I just put my money in some different mutual funds and let it sit there."

I really have no response to the above argument. Maybe I could reason that the above strategy is actually riskier than taking the 30 minutes or hour per day that one needs to keep track of real investment opportunities. The only thing that can change the mind of the mutual-fund advocate is witnessing their independent stock-investing friends achieve returns many times greater over the same time period of investing. One thing I would caution is to not try and increase returns by choosing a 'high-risk' category of equity mutual funds. That is a real way to lose money fast. Of course, the mutual fund investor will easily be able to point out stock investors that have taken a beating by choosing the wrong stocks to invest in.

To sum up, diversifying your investment is something you need to implement to one degree or another. Look at your tolerance for risk and act accordingly.

13

Goals

*The ants are a people not strong, yet they prepare
their meat in the summer.*

Prov. 30 25

Now that we have breached the topic of trading stocks and looked at
some of the opportunities that are available, it is my hope that the
reader may at this point be more open to taking a firm grip on their
financial future. Before rushing ahead, one has to examine closely their
starting point and where it is they want to go. If you ask the question,
"How much money do you need to retire?" You will get a wide range of
answers, from millions to a few hundred thousand. Sometimes it is recommended to have ten times your annual salary as a nest egg. For the
sake of simplicity, I like to use a target of $1 million of net assets outside
of personal property like real estate. This should be enough to provide a
secure income stream for my immediate family and myself and still
allow me to help others.

For some people, the concept of trying to get wealthy is inherently
wrong. For whatever reason, they feel that gaining wealth is either
immoral and or futile. I would like to address both these barriers.

Firstly, if a person is going to toil away for 25 years or so in the labor market, how much extra effort will it take to wisely set aside $100 or so off every paycheck into an investment account. The result of this tactic will relieve your relatives and society at large from having to support you in old age. We are not talking about robbing, cheating or clawing our way to the top of the corporate ladder. We are talking about accumulating a solid nest egg that grants us financial security all the while helping to finance the growth of Canadian industry.

At one time, this was the concept behind saving money in a bank. Industrious common folk would deposit their savings in return for interest, knowing that their saving was helping the growth of business, farmers and others that needed loans for expansion. Unfortunately today most businesses do not get money from banks. They get money from venture capitalists and investors. Sure they may have a credit line with a bank, but for the most part, banks don't want to risk lending to business when they can squeeze money out of every Canadian with a home or car loan. Banks also don't pay interest to savers like in the old days, but rather impose service charges. If Canadians want to be diligent and help invest in Canadian business, they should be saving/investing into solid Canadian businesses. This strategy will pay more interest than any bank.

Becoming financially independent is far from immoral. It is only by helping oneself that an individual will have the financial power to help those less fortunate in society who cannot help themselves. It is essentially the obligation of every Canadian with a sound mind to help themselves so that they CAN help others.

As far as the idea that becoming wealthy is futile, that claim is easily disputed by the results I have personally experienced and also by the results I have seen others accomplish in a remarkably short period of time. There are scores of Canadians quietly and methodically increasing their net worth exponentially while their next-door neighbors are oblivious to the opportunities available to them.

A person who says it can't be done is what is called a 'scoffer'. They are those that are quick to put down any aspirations with comments like, "Yeah right, you'll lose your shirt in the stock-market, that's all." Cubicles across the country are filled with scoffers. They are so much more comfortable with mediocrity that they quickly dismiss any ideas of getting ahead as a waste of time. To admit to the possibility of self-development is to admit to their own laziness and failures, a most unpleasant realization.

The fact of the matter is that for any positive-minded person that is willing to learn, making money in stocks is not only possible, but also actually kind of easy. It does not take any great ability in the areas of people skills, personal presentation, charisma or innate talent. It merely requires some basic training, practice and patience.

Once an individual believes in the possibility of getting ahead and is willing to put in the effort and time, he or she must set down in writing, specific goals as to where they would like to go financially. You need to be aware of your starting position. Simply set up a balance sheet like so:

CASH	$5,000
SELF DIRECT RRSP TRADING ACCOUNT	$15,000
PERSONAL LOAN DEBT	- $10,000
CREDIT CARD DEBT	- $10,000

The individual in the above scenario would have a net worth of zero, as the assets equal the liabilities. For your starting point, you can leave out long-term debt like your mortgage for now. Just look at your 'current' status. Secondly take a look at your cash flow status.

NET MONTHLY INCOME	$2000
- Rent/Mortgage	- $1000
- Loan Payment	- $150
- Credit Card Payment	- $150
- Misc Expenses	- $400

This table shows that the individual has positive cash flow of $300 per month. Once you realize your starting position, you can imagine where you would like to be in six months or one year. Your first goal setting exercise is **write down what you plan your net worth to be in one year**. Your goal must be written down on paper. If you just imagine a number, it will likely have no effect. There is something powerful about actually writing down an actual number on paper. This number must be **believable**; it should be a number that will cause you to stretch yourself to attain it. In the above example, a good written one-year goal would be a net worth of $25,000. Starting from zero, to reach $25,000 net worth would be a huge step towards financial independence but certainly achievable. It would be useless to set a goal of zero to $1 million in one year…remember to achieve your goal it must be believable.

Speaking from my own experience, I always wrote out my goals by hand and then typed them into the computer so I could print them out in the following format given below. I learned this basic form of goal setting from reading Maximum Achievement by Brian Tracy and I would highly recommend this book to anyone interested in goal setting and self-improvement. [7]

---

7. Maximum Achievement, Brian Tracy , Simon & Schuster 1993
Brian Tracy International, 462 Stevens Ave, Suite 202, Solana Beach, CA 92075
858-481-2977

Desire: Financial Independence

Belief: It is Possible!

Write it down: Specific Primary Goal: $xxx,xxx in liquid assets.

Determine how I will benefit from achieving this goal:

Write all the ways that reaching your goal will improve your life. More time with family, able to support specific charities, freedom to travel etc.

Analyze the starting point: From the balance sheet exercise above, write out your current net worth.

Monthly Targets: Prepare personal balance sheets at the end of every month to track your progress.

Date of Achievement: Set a specific deadline for when you will achieve your goal.

Identify objects that stand in my way:

Write down all the barriers to your goal such as excessive spending, using credit cards etc.

Identify additional knowledge or action required:

Write down current action items. Open trading account, get carry-forward loan, stock research etc.

Identify people whose co-operation I will require:

Write down list of those people whose help you will need; bank manager, co-workers, friends etc.

See the end result in your mind–Make a plan: Read over this list every morning and evening.

Persistence-Don't give up! Believe it! Achieve it!

You can print out the above or similar format on a one-page sheet of paper and hang it on the wall of your office or on your fridge, anywhere that you will see it on a regular basis as a reminder.

Once you have your goal written down, you will be able to consciously and unconsciously focus towards achieving it. I found the effect of written goals to be near miraculous in effectiveness. I hit my first one-year target almost to the penny. It had been a believable target but I had no real means for achieving it at the time it was written.

At the end of the year, I repeat the process by setting a new twelve-month target and verifying all the steps involved. The reward to effort ratio of this exercise is incalculable.

TRADING GOALS

Before placing any trade you should have written goals as to where you want to buy and sell. A common mistake when trading is to look at a stock and say, "Well XYZ Company is trading at $12 per share, if it dips down to $10 per share, I will buy." Firstly, you should be using the technical indicators we have already discussed to know when you are at a relative low point so that you can purchase shares confidently. Second, a trader would be better off to state, " Well XYZ Company is trading at $12 per share, if the shares go up and hit $14 per share I will buy." **You want to purchase shares that are rising not falling.** Intuitively this strategy does not feel good at all, but trust me, buy shares that are going up not down; your own experience will help you to understand this concept better than I can try and explain it.

Before placing a trade you absolutely must have a downside exit price. That is price below what you paid for the shares where you will take your loss and sell. The exception is when you are at the buy and hold stage where you are not concerned about temporary market downturns. It is at this stage where you may employ dollar cost averaging as well.

If you are looking for short-term trades (holding time usually 1 week to 1 month or so) you must assume that you are wrong before you trade! The stock market is counter-intuitive. What that means is that shares prices will usually move in the short term where you do not expect them to go. You should expect to be wrong 7 out of 10 times. By keeping your losses on your 7 losing trades to a minimum, you will come out ahead when your 3 winners make large gains. When you purchase a stock that starts to move in your favor, it is a lot easier to switch to a buy and hold strategy once you are in the black. I have often been in and out of stocks a couple of times before finally getting firmly in and holding for long term gains. The small losses incurred in 'getting settled' are insignificant compared to the overall long-term profits.

In summary, never underestimate the value of setting goals, in particular, written goals.

14

Motivation

The sluggard craves and gets nothing, but the desires of the diligent are fully satisfied.

Prov. 13 v 4

An investor must be motivated to achieve success. If discouragement sets in, the once hopeful investor becomes depressed to the point where the very thought of stocks causes a negative reaction in his or her demeanor. You can notice this if you ever casually ask a friend about stocks. If they have had bad experiences in the past, they will usually be totally opposed to any forms of stock investing. A conversation might go like this: "Hi Ted, I just purchased some shares of XYZ company and thought I would ask if you had ever heard of them before." Ted replies, "Naw, you're talking to the wrong person, I don't touch that kinda stuff. You may as well just throw darts at a dartboard to pick stocks these days." Obviously Ted has closed himself off from the opportunities inherent in investing and it would take a minor miracle for him to ever have a change of heart. Usually this type of response is indicative of a bad experience in the past

How do you, as an eager investor prevent the above situation from happening? Nothing succeeds like success and once you get a few profitable trades under your belt, you will probably never be short on motivation for quite some time. It is thus important to get off to a positive start. If you are beginning from ground zero, a good place to start is with the large cap companies listed in the chapter on Current Opportunities. Don't be concerned about purchasing shares in odd-lots (quantities less than 100 at a time). If you want to invest $500 in a company whose shares are trading at $50, don't try and save up $5000 before investing. Buy 10 shares now and keep on saving. Although you may pay more in commission, it will allow you to feel more connected to the market to have the shares in hand and also will have the effect of averaging out your purchase costs.

As an investor you should be getting monthly account statements for your investment accounts. You can also print out your own monthly bank statement from the Internet. This will give you a snapshot of your financial situation. If you currently do not do your banking online, I highly recommend it for convenience. Seeing your net worth grow is highly motivating. As soon as you have written goals and know your starting position, it will be quite difficult NOT to see significant changes start to take place in your financial position. Especially if starting at a negative net worth position, the realization of reaching break-even can be exhilarating. Reaching a net worth of $10,000 is better than winning the lottery! As Fred Young mentions in his book, How to Get Rich and Stay Rich: getting your first $10,000 is difficult, getting your next $10,000 is a little easier but almost as hard. Earning your first $100,000 is a lot of hard work but getting your next $100,000 is a lot easier. Earning your first $1,000,000 is extremely difficult but getting your second million is a snap! It took Fred Young until age 65 to retire with one million dollars after working for the Harris Bank in Chicago for 27 years and patiently investing all along. About four years after than he passed the two million mark. A couple years further along he was approaching the three million mark even after experiencing some significant market downturns.

What can we learn from Fred Young's experience? Getting your first $10,000 is the most important step! Don't forget to assess your financial position on a monthly basis, you will find this exercise to be one of the most motivating activities. It only takes an hour or so on the first of every month.

Try and keep company with positive people. If you are excited about investing, remember that most people will not understand your point of view, especially those with pre-conceived ideas. A lot of people will sum their opinion on the stock market with one sentence. "Stocks are too risky" or "The market is fixed". To have a simple negative view of stocks protects lazy people from having to understand something that they don't know about. It is a lot easier to dismiss the entire topic altogether than to be faced with the idea that maybe they were not altogether correct all these years. If that is the case, don't try and convince them otherwise but make sure their negative attitudes do not rub off on you.

A good way to keep motivated is by studying. Let's say the reader knows absolutely nothing about stocks or investing. There are ten books listed in the recommended reading section at the back of this book. If one were to read all 10 books (start with any book by Peter Lynch) it may take six months or a year; at the end of which, the reader would have a surprisingly solid understanding of many financial matters. The knowledge from these ten books alone would put you head and shoulders above most average investors. And there are many, many more good books out there. Most of this information is not taught in schools or university. Knowledge builds confidence and confidence will keep you motivated. At your own pace, always keep adding to your base of financial knowledge.

Study is also required in the area of motivation itself. Try and always be in the process of reading something motivational. Brian Tracy,

Anthony Robbins, Dr. Robert Anthony; these types of writers will provide you with a constant fueling of confidence in your ability to succeed.

It does not take any great natural talent to invest wisely, merely patience and discipline, qualities that are available to everyone.

15

Current Opportunities

He that tilleth his land shall have plenty of bread.

Prov.28 v 19

I would like to list for the reader, a group of Canadian technology stocks that are experiencing high growth and should provide positive returns in the near future. I will start with large cap (companies with a market capitalization of over 1 billion cdn) and also list smaller cap companies, which have more potential for explosive growth but will also carry more risk. Finally I listed some under-performing companies for contrast in the category of turn-around opportunities.

Are there solid companies in other industries that have potential for high growth? Absolutely. Many biotech companies have huge potential especially considering the aging population and recent advancements in genetic research. I simply prefer to focus on technology stocks due to the global demand for technological innovation. There are also many other good companies in both large and small cap categories that I have not listed here. I leave it to the reader to identify stocks not listed here that are as good or better investments. I have limited my selections for the sake of brevity and to avoid over-loading the reader with too many companies to look at. At the time of writing, I hold positions in Nortel Networks, Tundra Semiconductor, A.L.I. Technologies, Eiger Technology and OnX Inc.

Large Cap:

NT	Nortel Networks	MLT	Mitel
ATY	ATI Technologies	DSG	Descartes Systems Group
JDU	JDS Uniphase	CMS	C-MAC Industries
RIM	Research in Motion	CSN	Cognos
RCI.B	Rogers Communications	LSI	GSI Lumonics

Small Cap:

PME	Primetech Electronics Inc.	TUN	Tundra Semiconductor
ON	OnX Incorporated	MSD	Mosaid
RND	Rand Technology	CRY	Cryptologic Inc.
SGB	Stratos Global Corp	AXA	Eiger Technology
ALT	A.L.I. Technologies	BRT	Burntsand Inc.

Turn-Around Opportunities (high risk):

NBS	NBS Technologies	EIC	Eicon Technology
IVI	IVI Checkmate	E	Multiactive Software
CCW	Circuit World Corp	CSY	CSI Wireless Inc

By the time this book reaches the reader, there will no doubt be many new public companies from which to choose. To keep up to date on new stocks, make sure to check the Toronto Stock Exchange website under the heading "Recently Listed" every once in a while.

Pay special attention to Canadian public companies that you or your friends work for. Be aware of whether these companies are expanding their facilities, hiring new employees and or winning new contracts.

Don't try and get inside information or hot tips on takeovers; just keep aware of the general success or difficulties these companies may be facing.

Don't feel you have to be fully invested at all times. If you are using a buy and hold strategy with some of the companies listed above, be patient and don't be disturbed by the day-to-day fluctuations in the market. If you are placing a short-term trade, you also need to be patient as to when you feel conditions are right to buy. A good exercise is to practice by 'paper trading' for a while first. That is for your short term trades, write down on paper where you would buy and where you would sell without actually placing the trade. Be totally honest and set the same entry and exit targets as if you were actually trading in your account. This can be a tremendous help in understanding how effective your technical analysis may or may not be. Get practice at interpreting a variety of technical indicators and use the ones that you find to be the most helpful.

As your investment experience increases you will be able to stay on top of current opportunities in Canadian Public companies with ease. You will be able to interpret the business section of your newspaper more astutely. And you will develop an understanding and greater appreciation of current economic conditions.

Conclusions

Hopefully this book has served as an introduction to the opportunities for profit that exist in investing in Canadian public companies. It is by no means exhaustive in scope but rather is merely an effort to help those people with the fortitude to get started in the right direction. In my short investing experience, I have come to the following common-sense conclusions:

1) There are many Canadian public companies are world class in caliber. Both in terms of their products and as an investment to the purchaser of their shares.

2) There are many Canadian public companies that are essentially worthless as investments.

3) Saving is required for financial health.

4) Learning how to invest properly is a valuable exercise.

5) Emotional reactions in trading usually lead to bad trading decisions.

6) Investing without sufficient fundamental data usually leads to bad trading decisions.

7) A buy-and-hold strategy with quality growth stocks is highly effective and will outperform attempts at market timing.

8) Technical analysis despite inherent limitations can be useful in short-term trading.

9) Anyone capable of holding a job is probably capable of learning how to invest properly.

10) Success in investing is often directly related to a person's attitudes
and beliefs about investing.

I would liked to have gone into more depth in the areas of fundamental and technical analysis but again my intention was simply to
provide the reader a basic introduction and it is my hope that you
will be motivated to study these areas in more detail to your own
benefit. May you, as an independent Canadian investor, achieve great
success and be able to help yourself and help others.

Glossary

Ask (Offer)

The lowest price at which anyone is willing to sell a stock.

Annual Report

A publication, including financial statements and a report on operations, issued by a company to its shareholders at the company's fiscal year-end.

Averaging Down

Buying more of a security at a price that is lower than the price paid for the initial investment to reduce the average cost per unit.

Bear Market

A market in which stock prices are falling.

Bid

The highest price at which anyone is willing to buy a stock

Blue Chip Stocks

These are leading and nationally known companies whose common stocks offer a record of continuous dividend payments and other strong investment qualities.

Board Lot

A regular trading unit usually referring to 100 shares. The board lot size of a stock on the TSE could be 1000, 500, or 100 shares depending on the price of the stock. An investor buying or selling a board lot pays less commission rate than an investor buying or selling an odd lot.

Security Selling Price	Board Lot Size
$ 0.005 - 0.095	1,000 shares
$ 0.10 - $0.995	500 shares
$ 1.00 +	100 shares

Boiler Room Operation

A person or persons that sell shares over the phone out of an undisclosed location (like the boiler room of a building) that are worthless or fictitious and/or manipulated so that the buyer always loses their investment.

Bonds

Promissory notes issued by a corporation or government to its lenders, usually with a specified amount of interest for a specified length of time.

Breakout

A rise in a security's price above a resistance level (commonly its previous high price) or drop below a level of support (commonly the former lowest price.) A breakout is taken to signify a continuing move in the same direction. Can be used by technical analysts as a buy or sell indication.

Bull Market

A market in which stock prices are rising.

Capital gain or loss

The profit or loss you make when you sell an investment. Tax consequences may result.

Common Shares

Securities that represent part ownership in a company and generally carry voting privileges.

Day Order

An order that is valid only for the day it is entered. If the order is still outstanding when the market closes, it will be purged overnight.

Discounted

The market price of a share is said to have been 'discounted' when an event that is expected to happen, such as an increase in dividends or lower earnings, has been reflected in its price.

Diversification

Limiting investment risk by purchasing different types of securities from different companies.

Dividend

The part of a company's profits that you may receive if you are a shareholder of the company. Preferred shares earn a set dividend, while the dividends for common shares vary with the company's profits. Companies are under no legal obligation to pay dividends to their shareholders

Dollar Cost Averaging

Investing a fixed amount of dollars in a specific stock at regular set intervals over a period of time. Dollar cost averaging lowers the average cost per share when compared to purchasing a constant number of shares at set intervals. The investor buys more shares when the price is low and buys fewer shares when the price is high. Effective for a buy and hold strategy and when initially building up your investment account.

Dow Jones Industrial Average (DJIA)

The DJIA is composed of thirty companies that make up the Dow Jones Average. The calculation is done by adding the price of each of the thirty issues in the Index and dividing by a divisor. The DJIA is one of the most widely used stock market averages that appear in the financial pages of most newspapers.

Earnings Per Share (EPS)

Also referred to as Primary Earnings Per Share. Net income for the past 12 months divided by the number of common shares outstanding, as reported by a company. The company often uses a weighted average of shares outstanding over reporting term.

Equities

Common and preferred stocks, which represent a share in the owner-ship of a company.

Fixed income securities

Investments such as bonds and mortgage-backed securities that provide you with a regular income.

Growth Stock

The shares of companies that have enjoyed better-than-average growth over recent years and are expected to continue their climb.

Guaranteed Investment Certificate (GIC)

An investment where your money (usually at least $1,000) is deposited at a set rate of interest, for a fixed period of time. Basically you cannot take your money out early.

Income Stock

A security with a solid record of dividend payments, and which offers a dividend yield higher than the average common stock

Index

A statistical measure of the state of the stock market or economy, based on the performance of stocks. Examples are the TSE 300 Index or the Dow Jones Industrial Average.

Initial Public Offering

A company's first issue of shares to the general public.

Insider

All directors and senior officers of a company and those who may be presumed to have access to inside information concerning the company; also anyone owning more than 10% of the voting shares in a company.

Investment

Using your money to make money.

Investor Relations

A corporate function, combining finance, marketing and communications, to provide investors with accurate information about a company's performance and prospects.

Limit Order

An order to buy or sell stock at a specified price.

Listed Company / Public Company

A listed company is one whose shares are publicly traded on a stock exchange.

Long

A term signifying ownership of securities. For example, "I am long 100 shares of XYZ" means that the speaker owns 100 shares of XYZ company.

Margin

Brokers often lend money to investors for use in purchasing securities. The amount of money or securities that an investor must deposit with a broker to secure a loan from the broker is the margin.

Market Maker

A trader employed by a securities firm who is authorized and required by applicable self-regulatory organizations to maintain reasonable liquidity in securities markets by making firm bids or offers for one or more designated securities up to a specified minimum guaranteed fill.

Market Order

An order to buy or sell stock immediately at the best current price. Marginal Propensity to consume: The tendency people have to spend as their income rises. As income rises people increase their spending in direct proportion at a pace that they can't quite afford, keeping themselves perpetually in debt.

Mutual Fund

A fund managed by an individual or group who invests in stocks, bonds, options, money market instruments or other securities. Mutual fund units can be purchased through brokers or, in some cases, directly from the mutual fund company.

Odd-lot

A quantity of shares less than a board lot usually less than one hundred (see board lot). An odd-lot number of shares may be slightly more difficult to fill when buying or selling. There is no minimum number of shares that you must purchase at a time however commission charges may be proportionately higher when buying or selling only a few shares.

Open Order

An order that remains in the system longer than a single day

Paper profit

When the investments you hold are worth more than you paid for them. If you sell your investments for more than you paid for them, then you have a realized profit.

Penny stocks

Low-priced, generally risky shares selling at less than $1 per share.

Portfolio

Holdings of securities by an individual or institution. A portfolio may include various types of securities representing different companies as well as cash.

Profit-taking

Selling an investment to take a profit. The process of converting paper profits into cash.

Program Trading

Trades based on signals from computer programs, usually entered directly from the trader's computer to the market's computer system and executed automatically.

Prospectus

A legal document describing securities being offered for sale to the public. It must be prepared in accordance with provincial securities commission regulations.

Rally

A brisk rise in the general price level of the market or in the price of an individual stock.

Settlement Date

The date on which a securities buyer must pay for a purchase or a seller must deliver the securities sold. In general, settlement must be made on or before the third business day following the transaction date.

Share Repurchase

Program by which a corporation buys back its own shares in the open market. It usually is done when shares are undervalued. Since it reduces the number of shares outstanding and thus increases earnings per share, it tends to elevate the market value of the remaining shares held by stockholders.

Short Selling

The sale of stocks that the seller does not own. The seller is speculating that the price will fall, in the hope of later purchasing the same number of shares at a lower price, thereby making a profit. Short sellers must borrow the securities sold short in order to make proper settlement.

Short selling carries the risk of unlimited losses since shares can rise and keep on rising indefinitely.

Stock Split

A division of the outstanding shares of a corporation into a larger number of shares; by which each outstanding share entitles its owner to a pre-determined number of new shares. For example, in a two-for-one split, a shareholder with 100 shares valued at $50 each would exchange them for 200 shares at $25 each. Since this is done with all shares, each shareholder's equity in the company remains the same. This is often a sign of a growth stock. This increases number of shares available to investors and allows shares to be purchased at a lower cost per share. Companies that have had a serious drop in share price can declare a reverse stock split, thereby consolidating the number of shares outstanding, not a good thing for investors.

TSE 300 Composite Index

This index is a benchmark used to measure the price performance of the broad Canadian equity market.

Trading Halt

A trading halt (stops the buying and selling of a specific stock) is temporarily imposed by the TSE, usually due to a news announcement.

Trading Symbol

The symbol, usually one to three letters, is shorthand for the names of listed stocks.

Warrant

A certificate that gives the holder the right to buy the underlying security at a specified price for a specified time directly from the company.

About the Author

Patrick Doucette grew up in a typical hard-working Canadian family. Due to his parent's penchant for traveling, by the age of 18 he had resided in every Canadian Province except Manitoba and Saskatchewan.

Patrick studied Economics and Finance at Concordia University in Montreal where he received a Bachelor of Commerce Degree in 1990. He also studied at Carleton University in Ottawa, receiving a Bachelor of Arts Degree in Philosophy in 1993. He is a graduate of the Canadian Securities Course, a shodan and life member of Shotokan Karate of America and member of MENSA Canada.

Patrick has been employed in various cubicle environment positions from 1993 to 1999.

He currently is semi-retired and resides in Toronto, Ontario.

If you are interested in having Patrick speak to your organization or have questions or comments, he can be reached via e-mail at pawwnn@yahoo.com

Appendix A

Useful websites for Canadian investors.

www.dbc.com

www.globeinvestor.com

www.finance.yahoo.com

www.fin-info.com

www.tse.com

www.stockhouse.ca

www.canada.bigcharts.com

www.multex.multexinvestor.com

www.carlsononline.com

www.cbsmarketwatch.com

www.canoe.ca/Money/

LIST OF CANADIAN ONLINE BROKERAGES TO SET UP A TRADING ACCOUNT

www.tdwaterhouse.ca	Toronto Dominion Bank
www.actiondirect.com	Royal Bank
www.bmoinvestorline.com	Bank of Montreal
www.investorsedge.cibc.com	Canadian Imperial Bank of Commerce
www.sdbi.com	Bank of Nova Scotia

www.investnet.com	National Bank
www.hsbcinvestdirect.com	HSBC Invest Direct
www.canada.etrade.com	E-Trade Canada
www.enorthern.com	eNorthern
www.schwabcanada.com	Charles Schwab Canada
www.sunsecurities.com	Sun Life Securities

Appendix B

Technical Indicators:

Accumulation/Distribution

A volume-weighted calculation that takes into account the range at which an issue is traded. Interval volume is either added (closes up) or subtracted (closes down) from the total volume.

Average True Range

An average of a stock's price range over n-intervals.

Bollinger Bands

Consists of a center line and a set of channel lines. The center line is an n-interval moving average. The channel lines are placed at n-standard deviations above and below the center line.

Envelope Channel

Consists of a center line and a set of channel lines. The center is an n-interval exponential moving average. The channel lines are placed on both sides of the centerline at a percentage distance away.

Exponential Moving Average

Similar to the weighted moving average, but all data is taken into account in the average.

Linear Regression

Consists of a centerline and a set of channel lines. The center line, the linear regression, is generated by a least squares calculation. The channels lines are placed on both sides of the center line at a percentage distance away.

Momentum

An indicator that is calculated by taking a price from n-intervals ago and subtracting it from the current interval's price.

Money Flow

A Volume-weighted version of the relative strength index, but instead of using up closes vs. down closes, Money Flow compares the current interval's average price to the previous interval's average price and then weighs the average price by volume to calculate money flow. The ratio of the summed positive and negative money flows are then normalized to be on a scale of 0-100.

Moving Average Convergence Divergence (MACD)

Consists of two lines. The first line, a MACD line, is the difference between the long-term moving average and the short-term moving average. The second line, a signal line, is a short term moving average of the MACD line.

On Balance Volume

On balance volume is an accumulation of volume where: the current interval's volume is added to the total if the stock closes up, and today's volume is subtracted from the total if the stock closes down.

Price Oscillator

An indicator that displays the difference between a slow and fast period subtracting it from the current interval's price.

Rate of Change

An indicator that calculates the market's change from the current interval's price vs. price n-intervals ago. The result is a percentage.

Relative Strength Index

A ratio of close-up intervals vs. close-down intervals over n-intervals.

Simple Moving Average

Average of last n-interval's close prices.

Stochastic–(%K)

Determines where the most recent closing price is in relation to the price range for an n-interval period. Two lines are plotted, a "fast" line (%K) and a "slow" line (%D). %D is a 3-period moving average of %K. My own long-term back-tested studies have indicated an optimum predictive stochastic using 14–16 days as the n-interval period.

Fast %K=100 x {current close–lowest low / highest high–lowest low}

Slow %K=3 period moving average of Fast % K

Buy indications (stochastic below 20) tend to be more accurate in stocks that are in a general up-trend and sell indications (stochastic above 80) tend to be more accurate in stocks that in an overall downtrend.

The most accurate stochastic interpretation is to look for price divergence. When price patterns are making higher tops while the stochastic indicator is making lower tops, this is called bearish divergence. As the name implies, this is a sell signal. Conversely, when the price pattern is making lower bottoms and the stochastic indicator is making higher bottoms, this is bullish divergence.

Weighted Moving Average

Similar to a simple moving average, but gives more weight to current data in the n-interval average calculation.

William's %R

%R is an index that determines where the most recent closing price is in relation to the price range for an n-interval period.

Recommended Reading List

1) The Golden Fleece (out of print)
Walter Stewart   McClelland & Stewart Inc. 1992

2) Rampaging Bulls
Alexander Tadich   Elan Publishing 1992

3) Beating the Street
Peter Lynch   Simon & Schuster 1994

4) Getting Started in Stocks
Alvin D. Hall   Wiley, John & Sons 1998

5) Building Wealth in the 90's
Gordon Pape   Prentice Hall Canada 1992

6) Reminiscences of a Stock Operator
Edwin Lefévre   John Wiley & Sons 1994

7) Maximum Achievement
Brian Tracy   Simon & Schuster 1993

8) How to Get Rich and Stay Rich (out of print)
Fred J. Young   Lifetime Books 1992

9) How to Make Money in Stocks

William J. O'Neil   McGraw-Hill 1994

10) One Up on Wall Street

Peter Lynch   Simon & Schuster 2000

Printed in the United States
18469LVS00006B/301-306